Hawaii's Best Hiking Trails

by Robert Smith

Wilderness Press
BERKELEY

First Edition 1982
SECOND Edition 1985

Copyright © 1982, 1985 by Robert Smith
Maps by Kevin G. Chard
Front-cover photo by Ed Cooper
Photos by the author
Design by Thomas Winnett

Library of Congress Card Catalog Number 85-040706
International Standard Book Number 0-89997-058-3

Manufactured in the United States

Published by Wilderness Press
              2440 Bancroft Way
              Berkeley CA 94704
Write for free catalog

Library of Congress Cataloging-in-Publication Data

Smith, Robert, 1934-
  Hawaii's best hiking trails.

  Includes index.
  Hiking—Hawaii—Guide-books. 2. Hawaii—
Description and travel—1981-   —Guide-books.
I. Title.
GV199.42.H3S64 1985   919'.69   85-40706
ISBN 0-89997-058-3 (pbk.)

Dedication

Hi'ipoi i ka 'aina aloha
(Cherish the beloved land)

Acknowledgements

Many people made significant contributions to this book. In Hawaii, I am indebted to Ruth Wryn and Vi Saffery of the Wailuku Public Library and to Gail Bartholomew, librarian at Maui Community College, each of whom cheerfully responded to my numerous requests. A number of Hawaii State officials offered information and expertise. Robert Hobdy, Maui forester; Ralph E. Daehler, Kauai District Forester; and Mac Hori, State Park Supervisor on Kauai, were particularly helpful. Thanks to Bill Crane for his companionship on many of the hikes and for his knowledge and helpful suggestions. A very special "mahalo" to Nobuko Yamada on Maui; Roy, Carol, Shari, Frances and Mac Fujioka on Kauai; and Vonnie Harwick on Oahu for their hospitality. On the mainland two people gave their time and professional advice. Louis Mellencamp assisted with the photos in this book, and Fred Samia read the manuscript.

Without the support of my family this book would not have been possible. Nancy, my wife, labored long hours to type and correct the manuscript, and my children, Cheryl Anne, Miles and Jason, provided campanionship on many of the trails and performed numerous tasks.

Contents

Introduction

Hawaii—The 50th State

"I'm not going to Hawaii; it's overcommercialized; it's like Los Angeles with coconut trees." These are statements frequently overheard on the mainland by people who are unknowing. Admittedly, some of the tourist centers on each of the islands have boomed in recent years, and much sand and open space have been replaced with lumber and concrete in the form of shopping centers, condominiums, hotels, bars, souvenir shops, and the like. However, there remains a nearly pristine Hawaii, a wild and free Hawaii, an alluring and enchanting Hawaii, and an exciting and romantic Hawaii. It's still there, only you have to know where to find it! It is the purpose of this book to reveal some of those places in Hawaii which soothe the body and calm the spirit— those special places which for sometimes unexplainable reasons have an impact on our lives. But with each discovery there is the responsibility to protect and preserve—to "Hi'ipoi i ka 'aina aloha (cherish the beloved land).

In 1980, 3.36 million people visited Hawaii. Some were looking for the dance halls and night clubs along Kalakaua Avenue on Waikiki, some for the slower, more relaxed pace found on the neighbor islands, and some for the beautiful and primitive life in Kalalau or Waimanu Valley. Whatever they sought, they probably found it because they keep coming back to what Mark Twain once described as "the loveliest fleet of islands that lies anchored in any ocean." The "fleet" is made up of 132 islands, although only seven are inhabited and only six may be visited (Niihau is privately owned). A little larger than the state of Connecticut, the 50th state joined the union in 1959 as the only state where no single ethnic group is in the majority, which accounts for a marvelous blend of races and cultures that serves as an example of relatively harmonious living. Recently, Caucasians became the single largest minority group, followed closely by people of Japanese ancestry, with Hawaiian and part-Hawaiian a distant third. Then add the Filipinos, Chinese, Koreans, Blacks, Samoans and a dash of European groups and you have Hawaii—almost. The last ingredient is "aloha"—a word that cannot be defined. Some will say it means "hello" or "goodby" or "love." But "aloha" is a state of mind; it's a feeling of affection and regard that one person has for another be he longtime friend or malihini (newcomer); it's that inner force that causes one person to care for and to share with friends and strangers alike; it's that spiritual quality that binds "brahs" and visitors; in short, it is "aloha." Don't listen to those who say it no longer exists in Hawaii. It's still there. You're likely to find this spirit of brotherhood in meetings with local people in the tourists shops, on the beach, or on the trail. But remember, it has to be reciprocal.

While Hawaiians are justifiably proud of their aloha spirit, there are other unique and distinguishable characteristics in which they take pride. For example, Hawaii is not only the youngest of the 50 states, by also the youngest in terms of creation. It is believed that the islands began to be formed about 25 million years ago by eruptions from a 2000-mile fault at the bottom of the Pacific. Geologically speaking, Hawaii is still an infant and is still growing, witnessed by Mauna Loa on the "Big Island," the world's largest active volcano, and by Kilauea, also on the "Big Island," the most active volcano in the world. Additionally, the 50th state boasts the wettest place on the earth (Mt. Waialeale, Kauai, average of 486 inches of rain annually). Hawaiians boast that theirs is the longest state, stretching 1523 miles from the eastern tip of Hawaii, the Big Island, to the tiny speck known as Kure Atoll. But the most alluring characteristic of Hawaii is the climate. Tropical Hawaii has a combination of cooling trade winds and equable temperatures in the vicinity of 75°. For example, in Honolulu, the highest recorded temperature was 88° and the lowest 57°. The highest temperature ever recorded in the state was 100°. In such a setting, outdoor experiences attract thousands each year.

Safe Hiking in Hawaii

Hiking and backpacking have increased in popularity in recent years in Hawaii not only, I suspect, because they are an inexpensive way to travel, but also they are a different way to experience a place. In Hawaii, outdoor experiences are outstanding; however, the outdoors-person should be aware of a number of problems. For one, violent actions against hikers and campers, while remaining low percentagewise considering the numbers who are taking to the trail, have increased. As any community grows and urban centers develop, the ills of city life, including violence and crime, follow. Consequently, you are cautioned never to hike or camp alone, particularly females. As a general rule, the farther you hike and camp away from populated areas, the safer your experience is likely to be. NEVER leave valuables unprotected. I always carry a daypack containing those items which I cannot afford to lose—wallet, airline ticket, camera—and I carry it everywhere. Yes, even there!

Another problem facing the hiker in Hawaii is the lack of trailhead signs and trail markers. Most of the trails contained in this book are well-defined, but most are not marked. Consequently, I provide detailed directions to the trailhead and a trail narrative that makes the trail easy to follow. I have included a wide selection of trips from short, easy family walks to long, difficult hikes. Most of the hikes are on public lands where well-maintained trails await the hiker. Other hikes are on private land—pineapple and sugar-cane holdings—and some are on military reservations. In spite of the time and effort required to secure permission from property owners, I have included these worthy hikes. I have not included areas from which hikers are forbidden by law (protected watershed) or where the terrain is dangerous and unsafe even though local people may boast of their adventures into these places. Each year numerous injuries and some fatalities occur where people have hiked in spite of the prohibition. Good judgment and a regard for the time-tested rules of hiking are good protection.

Hikers and campers are always relieved to learn that there are no poisonous snakes nor is there any poison ivy or poison oak in Hawaii. Poisonous centipedes and scorpions are found at low elevations, but I have never seen any in the wilderness, only in urban areas. The two biggest pests in Hawaii are the mosquito and the cockroach. While neither is fatal to man, both are very troublesome. They can make an outdoor experience disagreeable unless precautions are taken. You will have to live with the cockroach, but all of the mosquito lotions and sprays seem to provide effective protection. Due to the wet climate, be prepared to make frequent applications.

In order to ensure a safe and enjoyable experience and to protect the environment, remember:

1. Do not hike alone.
2. Many Hawaiian trails are wet and slippery, and the terrain is loose and brittle.
3. Contrary to popular belief, it is not possible to live off the land. Carry your own food.
4. Although some fruits are available, never eat or taste unknown fruits or plants.
5. Carry your own water or purify water from streams.
6. A tent with a rain fly ensures comfortable and dry nights.
7. Carry your trash out.
8. Bury personal wastes away from streams.
9. Firewood in most places is not available or is too wet for use. Carry a stove for cooking.
10. Darkness sets in right after sunset.

Using This Book

In planning a hike, the reader is advised to consult the Hiking Chart below in order to give due consideration to driving time, hiking time, and the clothing and supplies necessary. I have rated all the hikes and placed them in one of four categories. A "family" rated hike is for those who are looking for short, easy hikes. The "hardy family" class-ification requires a degree of effort and sound physical condition. Both the strenuous and the difficult hikes require a measure of endurance, since they are longer and most of them involve a considerable gain in altitude. They also require good footwear and more equipment.

Obviously, hiking time varies from person to person, depending on such things as pace and the extent to which one chooses to linger for lunch and to swim where pools exist. The time noted in the Hiking Chart is based on a leisurely pace. Trail distance is based either on an exact measurement or on an approximation with the aid of a topographic map.

Elevation gain or loss is cited in the Hiking Chart and preceding each trail narrative when the gain or loss is at least 500 feet. The gain or loss in elevation is from the trailhead or starting point cited in the narrative. Where the return trip is over the same trail, a like amount of loss or gain will be encountered. Where an alternative return route may be taken from trail's end, you will need to consult the trail narrative to determine the total elevation gain or loss for your entire trip. On the Hiking Chart, preceding the number of feet, "G" means gain and "L" means loss.

Driving time and mileage cited are based on the posted speed limit and are measured from a major point on each island. Specific driving instructions precede each hike description.

Only two islands—Oahu and Hawaii—have good reli-able public transportation systems. For each hike on those islands I have included bus directions to the trailhead. Use the bus; it is both inexpensive and reliable. If you plan to rent a car for transportation, I suggest that you do not volunteer the information to the rental agency that you are going to hike or camp. Most agencies will not rent vehicles to campers because they are concerned about breakdowns in the back-country and break-ins at the trailhead.

The equipment noted on the Hiking Chart is minimal for hiking enjoyment. As a rule, however, I always carry water, food and a first-aid kit. Although the choice between tennis shoes and hiking boots for some hikes is listed as optional, I prefer hiking boots in most cases. Obviously, your feet are an important consideration in hiking since it is common, on an island that has experienced extensive volcanic activity, to have volcanic ash or rock underfoot. Usually, the choice of shorts or long pants is optional, except where the brush is thick or when the weather requires warmer clothing.

Drinking water is available from streams in many areas, but it should be boiled or treated, since cattle, pigs and goats may share the water supply. To avoid the chance of illness, carry one quart of water per person. In many areas, firewood is at a premium. A small, light, reliable backpacking stove is a convenience and a comfort if you plan to cook out.

Before each hike description you will find the hike rating, trail features, hiking distance and time, specific driving instructions, instructions for getting there by bus and intro-ductory notes. On some hikes it is necessary to walk on private property. Information and addresses are provided so that you can secure permission in advance. Permission is usually readily granted either over the telephone or in person when you sign a liability waiver.

In the trail narrative I usually mention the flora and fauna to be seen along the way, especially the unusual and the unique, in an effort to add to your hiking enjoyment. But I don't mention everything, and you may wish to buy one of several guides to plants and animals of the islands, available at many stores.

Preceding each trail narrative is a map that will help you find the trailhead and to locate trail highlights. The maps show many features of the hikes as well as campsites.

Hiking Chart

	Hike Rating				Trail Time			Equipment					Features				
	Family	Hardy family	Strenuous	Difficult	Distance (miles)	Time (hours)	Gain/loss (feet)	Rain gear	Boots	Tennis shoes	Carry water	Take food	Swimming	Waterfalls	Views	Historical sites	Fruits
HAWAII																	
1 Hawaii Volcanoes Nat. Pk.																	
Mauna Loa Summit				X	18.9	3-4 days	+7015		X		X	X			X	X	
Crater Rim			X		**11.6**	day		X	X		X	X			X	X	
Halemaumau		X			3.2	2			X		X	X			X	X	
Byron Ledge			X		2.5	1½			X		X	X			X	X	
Kilauea Iki			X		4.0	2½			X		X	X			X	X	
Thurston Lava Tube	X				0.3	¼				X						X	
Devastation	X				0.6	¼				X					X	X	
Sandalwood	X				0.7	¼				X					X	X	
Sulfur Bank	X				0.3	¼				X					X		
Halape				X	7.2	6	−3000		X		X	X	X		X	X	
Hilina Pali				X	6.4	4	−2000		X		X	X			X		
Kau Desert				X	19.9	day	−4000		X		X	X			X	X	
Mauna Iki			X		8.8	8			X		X	X			X	X	
Puu Loa Petroglyphs		X			1.0	¾				X					X	X	
Naulu		X			2.0	1			X		X	X			X		
Napau			X		7.0	4			X		X	X			X	X	
2 Akaka Falls	X				**0.7**	½				X				X	X		
3 Waipio/Waimanu Valleys				X	9.0	7	±1000	X	X		X	X	X	X	X	X	X
4 Puako Petroglyphs		X			1.0	1				X	X					X	
5 Captain Cook Monument			X		2.5	2	−500		X		X	X	X		X	X	X
6 Mauna Kea Summit				X	6.0	5	+4176		X		X	X			X	X	
KAUAI																	
7 Kalalau				X	10.8	8	+2000	X	X		X	X	X	X	X	X	X
8 Nonou Mountain		X															
East side		X			2.0	1½	+1250	X	X		X	X			X		
West side		X			1.5	1	+1000	X	X		X	X			X		
9 Keahua																	
Keahua Arboretum	X				**0.5**	½				X			X				X
Moalepe		X			2.5	1½		X	X		X	X			X		X
Kuilau Ridge		X			2.1	1½		X	X		X	X	X		X		X
10 Kokee State Park/ Waimea Canyon																	
Berry Flat	X				1.0	½		X		X	X	X					
Puu Ka Ohelo	X				0.3	¼		X		X	X						X
Canyon			X		1.7	2	−800	X	X		X	X	X	X	X		
Cliff	X				0.1	1/6		X	X						X		
Ditch			X		3.5	4		X	X		X	X		X	X		X

Mileages in boldface are for loops.

Hiking Chart	Hike Rating				Trail Time			Equipment					Features				
	Family	Hardy family	Strenuous	Difficult	Distance (miles)	Time (hours)	Gain/loss (feet)	Rain gear	Boots	Tennis shoes	Carry water	Take food	Swimming	Waterfalls	Views	Historical sites	Fruits
Iliau Nature Loop	X				0.3	¼			X						X	X	
Kaluapuhi		X			1.7	1½		X		X	X	X					X
Koaie Canyon				X	3.0	2		X	X		X	X	X	X	X	X	X
Kukui			X		2.5	2	−2000	X	X		X	X	X	X	X		X
Waialae Canyon			X		0.3	½		X	X		X	X	X		X		
Waimea Canyon			X		1.5	2		X	X		X	X	X	X	X		
Alakai Swamp			X		3.4	3		X	X		X	X			X		
Awaawapuhi			X		3.3	3	−1600	X	X		X	X			X		
Honopu			X		2.5	2½	−1500	X	X		X	X			X		
Kawaikoi Stream		X			2.5	1½		X	X		X		X				X
Nualolo			X		3.7	3	−1500	X	X		X	X			X		
Pihea			X		3.3	3		X	X		X	X			X		
LANAI																	
11 **Munro**																	
Munro			X		8.8	day	+1400	X	X		X	X			X		X
North Hauola			X		2.0	1½	−1500	X	X		X	X			X		
Kaiholena Gulch			X		3.3	2	+1050	X	X		X	X			X		X
12 **Shipwreck Beach**	X	X	X		0-8	½ per mile				X	X	X	X		X	X	
MAUI																	
13 **Keane Arboretum**		X			1.3	1½		X		X	X	X	X				X
14 **Waianapanapa State Park**		X			3.0	2			X		X	X	X		X	X	
15 **Waimoku Falls**		X			2.5	2		X	X		X	X	X	X	X	X	X
16 **Haleakala National Park**			X			See text		X	X		X	X			X	X	
17 **Skyline**			X		8.0	4	−3800		X		X	X			X	X	
18 **Polipoli Park**																	
Redwood		X			1.7	1	−900	X	X		X	X			X	X	X
Tie		X			0.5	½	−500	X	X		X	X					
Plum		X			2.3	2		X	X		X	X			X	X	X
Polipoli	X				0.6	½		X	X		X				X		
Haleakala Ridge	X				1.6	1	−600	X	X		X	X			X		
Boundary		X			4.4	4		X	X		X	X			X	X	X
Waiohuli		X			1.4	1½	−800	X	X		X	X			X		
19 **Iao Valley**																	
Tableland		X			2.0	1½	+500	X	X		X	X	X	X	X		X
Iao Stream	X				1.0	½				X			X				X
Poohahoahoa Stream			X		3.0	2		X		X	X	X	X	X			X
Nakalaloa Stream			X		2.5	2		X		X	X	X	X	X			X
20 **Cross above Wailuku**		X			1.0	1	+1000		X		X	X			X		
21 **Waihee Ridge**			X		2.7	3	+1500	X	X		X	X		X	X		X

Hiking Chart

	Hike Rating				Trail Time			Equipment					Features				
	Family	Hardy family	Strenuous	Difficult	Distance (miles)	Time (hours)	Gain/loss (feet)	Rain gear	Boots	Tennis shoes	Carry water	Take food	Swimming	Waterfalls	Views	Historical sites	Fruits
MOLOKAI																	
22 **Haiawa Valley**		X			2.0	1				X	X	X	X	X	X	X	X
23 **Kalaupapa**			X		2.0	1½	−1600		X		X	X	X			X	X
24 **Molokai Forest Reserve**																	
Hanalilolilo			X		3.0	2	+500	X	X		X	X		X	X		X
Puu Kolekole			X		2.5	2	+800	X	X		X	X			X		X
OAHU																	
25 **Diamond Head**	X				0.7	1	+550			X	X				X	X	
26 **Makiki/Tantalus**																	
Kanealole	X				0.7	½	+500		X		X				X		X
Nahuina		X			0.6	½	−600		X		X				X		
Makiki Valley	X				1.1	1			X		X				X		
Maunalaha	X				0.7	½	−555		X		X				X		X
Moleka		X			0.5	½			X		X				X		X
Ualakaa	X				0.6	½			X		X				X		
Manoa Cliffs		X			3.0	2	+500	X	X		X	X			X		X
Puu Ohia		X			2.0	1½	+500	X	X		X	X			X		X
27 **Manoa Falls**	X				0.8	1	+800		X		X		X	X			X
Aihualama		X			1.4	1½		X	X		X	X			X		X
28 **Lanipo**			X		3.0	3	+1600		X		X	X			X		
29 **Hanauma Bay**																	
Koko Head	X				1.0	½				X	X				X		
Koko Crater		X			1.0	1	+1000		X		X	X			X	X	
Blowhole		X			2.0	1½				X	X		X		X		
30 **Kahana Valley**	X				**4.5**	2½			X		X	X	X			X	X
31 **Sacred Falls**	X				2.2	1½			X		X	X	X	X			X
32 **Hauula Valley**																	
Hauula	X				**2.5**	1½	+600		X		X				X		
Maakua Gulch		X			3.0	3	+1100		X		X	X	X	X			
Papali	X				**2.5**	2	+800		X		X	X			X		
33 **Aiea Loop**	X				**4.8**	3		X	X		X	X			X		X
34 **Waimano**				X	7.1	4	+1600	X	X		X	X	X		X		X
35 **Manana**				X	6.0	4	+1700	X	X		X	X	X		X		X
36 **Dupont**				X	4.0	5	+3800	X	X		X	X			X		
37 **Kuaokala**			X		**4.5**	3	+500		X		X	X			X	X	X

Mileages in boldface are for loops.

Camping

Take a tent to Hawaii and camp out and you will save half the cost of a vacation in paradise and, if living in the out-of-doors is pleasurable to you, you will have the time of your life. What can be better than free campgrounds (only county campgrounds—except Oahu—charge a fee), beach camping with an overnight low temperature in the 70's and sunsets and sunrises that stir the senses? In the following pages, I have shown all the national-park, state-park, county, and private campgrounds on the maps and I have provided information concerning reservations and permits for camping on each island. As a general rule, I recommend the national-park and state-park campgrounds for not only are they the best maintained, but also they are free. For those who do not wish to camp but wish to keep expenses as low as possible, I suggest that you use the national-park and state-park house-keeping cabins, which are available on all the islands except Oahu and which cost only a few dollars per person per night. Information on them is provided for each island. However, since the cabins are popular with local people, make reservations early. Avoid camping areas in or near population centers, for in them all the ills of urban living are present such as thievery, vandalism, drunkenness, and the chance of personal injury. DO NOT camp alone and do not leave valuables and equipment unattended or unprotected.

Food and Equipment

The following equipment is recommended for day hikes.

> Day pack
> Hiking boots, strong shoes or tennis shoes
> Canteen, quart size (one per person)
> First-aid kit
> Scout or Swiss Army knife
> Insect repellent
> Shorts
> Bathing suit
> Sunburn lotion and/or preventive
> Sun glasses
> Whistle for each child

    Camera and film
    Hat
Optional:
    Poncho or raingear
    Towel
    Waterproof matches
    Flashlight

Planning and preparation are particularly important for the backpacker. The following equipment is recommended for overnight hikes and for campers.

General Equipment:
    Frame and pack
    Lightweight sleeping bag or blanket
    Tube tent or nylon tent with rain fly—rain is common in most areas
    Plastic ground cover—the ground is damp in most areas
    Sleep pad
    Canteen, quart size
    Scout or Swiss Army knife
    Flashlight
    40 feet of nylon cord
    First-aid kit
Cooking Gear:
    Backpack stove
    Fuel
    Cooking pots
    Sierra cup
    Waterproof matches
Clothing:
    Poncho or raingear—A MUST
    Pants
    Shorts and/or bathing suit
    Hat or bandana
    Underwear
    Socks
    Hiking boots
Toilet Articles:
    Soap (biodegradable)
    Toothbrush/powder-paste
    Part-roll toilet paper
    Chapstick
    Comb
    Washcloth and towel
    Insect repellent
    Sunburn lotion or preventive
Miscellaneous:
    Sun glasses
    Camera and film
    Plastic bags
    Fishing gear

Hawaiian Made Easy

For your interest, throughout the text wherever a Hawaiian place name is used, I have provided a literal translation if possible. In many instances, Hawaiian names have multiple meanings and even the experts sometimes disagree over literal meanings. The meanings given here are based on the best information available and on the context in which a name is used. As students of the environment, the Hawaiians had a flair for finding the most expressive words to describe their physical surroundings.

Most visitors are reluctant to try to pronounce Hawaiian words. But with a little practice and a knowledge of some simple rules, you can develop some language skill and add to your Hawaiian experience. Linguists regard Hawaiian as one of the most fluid and melodious languages of the world. There are only 12 letters in the Hawaiian alphabet: five vowels, a, e, i, o, u, and seven consonants, h, k, l, m, n, p, w. Hawaiian is spelled phonetically. Correct pronunciation is easy if you do not try to force English pronunciation onto the Hawaiian language. Vowel sounds are simple: a=ah; e=eh; i=ee; o=oh; and u=oo. Consonant sounds are the same as in English with the exception of w. Rules for w are not adhered to with any consistency by local people. Generally, w is pronounced "w" at the beginning of a word and after a. For example, Waimea is pronounced "Wai-may-ah" and wala-wala is "wah-lah-wah-lah." Hawaiians also usually pronounce w as "w" when it follows o or u: auwaha is "ah-oo-wah-hah," and hoowali is "hoh-oh-wah-lee." When w is next to the final letter of a word, it is variably pronounced "w" or "v"; Wahiawa is "wah-he-ah-wa," but Hawi is "ha-vee." Listen to the locals for their treatment of this letter. Finally, since the Hawaiian language is not strongly accented, the visitor will probably be understood without employing any accent.

Hawaii

The Island

"Here today, gone tomorrow" is applied or misapplied to a variety of situations. It might well be the motto of the Island of Hawaii. Certainly no other island in the Hawaiian chain and perhaps no other place on earth experience such dramatic and spectacular changes in such short periods of time. The "Big Island"—sometimes the "Orchid Island" or the "Volcano Island"—is the site of Mauna Loa, the world's largest active volcano and the largest single mountain on earth. In addition to Mauna Loa's frequent eruptions, another reason for all the change is the active shield volcano, Kilauea, in whose caldera Pele, the legendary and mischievous goddess of volcanoes, is said to reside. Kilauea, the "drive-in volcano," is a place where volcanic eruptions and lava flows can be viewed safely from an automobile or even more closely on foot.

With every eruption, the spewing lava alters the island in some way. Roads are overcome by the flowing lava, hiking trails are covered by ash or pumice, sometimes homes are destroyed, infrequently lives are lost, and, on occasion, new land is added to the state. For example, during an eruption in 1960, lava flowed into the sea and added 500 acres of land to the east side of the island. Thus, Hawaii was now 500 feet closer to California!

The largest (4038 square miles) of the Hawaiian Islands, Hawaii was formed by the building of five volcanoes. In the north, the now-extinct Kohala volcano is the oldest, rising to 5505 feet. Its peaks have been eroded to deep, precipitous valleys. Hualalai volcano (8251 feet) in the west last erupted in 1801 and is considered dormant. Towering, majestic Mauna Kea volcano dominates central Hawaii and at 13,796 feet is the highest peak on the island. Snow and winter sports are popular on its slopes. The remaining two volcanoes

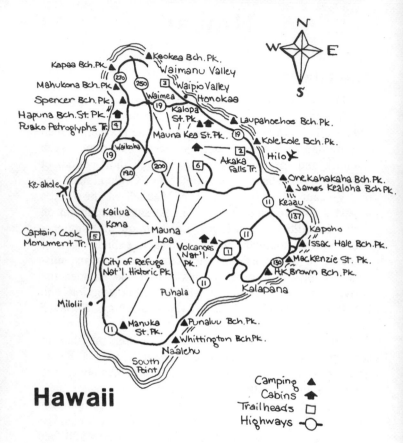

Kapaa Bch. Pk.
Mahukona Bch. Pk.
Spencer Bch. Pk.
Hapuna Bch. St. Pk.
Puako Petroglyphs Tr.
Keokea Bch. Pk.
Waimanu Valley
Waipio Valley
Waimea   Honokaa
Kalopa
St. Pk.
Laupahoehoe Bch. Pk.
Mauna Kea St. Pk.
Kolekole Bch. Pk.
Waikoloa
Akaka
Falls Tr.
Hilo
Ke-ahole
Onekahakaha Bch. Pk.
James Kealoha Bch. Pk.
Kailua
Kona
Mauna
Loa
Keaau
Captain Cook
Monument Tr.
Kapoho
Issac Hale Bch. Pk.
MacKenzie St. Pk.
City of Refuge
Nat'l. Historic Pk.
Volcanoes
Nat'l.
Pk.
H. K. Brown Bch. Pk.
Kalapana
Puhala
Milolii
Manuka
St. Pk.
Punaluu Bch. Pk.
Whittington Bch. Pk.
Naalehu
South
Point

Camping   ▲
Cabins   ♦
Trailheads   □
Highways   ○

Hawaii

command most of the attention because of frequent volcanic activity. Mauna Loa (13,677 feet) is the world's largest active volcano, and Kilauea, while a mere 4077 feet, has been the site of the most recent eruptions on the island.

Hawaii is about five times the size of any other island in the chain: 93 miles long, 76 miles wide and 318 miles around. One can drive completely around the island on good surfaced roads, a convenience not found on the other "neighbor" islands—Maui, Kauai, Molokai and Lanai.

Historically, Hawaii is believed to be the first island reached by Polynesian settlers, about 750 A.D. It is the birthplace of Kamehameha the Great, who conquered and unified the islands in the late 18th century. It is also the place where Captain James Cook was killed after he "discovered" the islands and introduced Western culture. However, perhaps the most notable resident is Pele, the goddess of volcanoes, who is said to reside in Halemaumau, Kilauea's fire pit.

In recent years Hawaii has competed with Maui for second place behind Oahu for tourists. Backpacks are conspicuous at the baggage counters as more and more visitors seek to discover a Hawaii different from the standard tourist fare.

Camping

Campgrounds on Hawaii range from adequate to good and contain most of the amenities. The price is right: all but county campgrounds are free. This book's camping/hiking map of the island locates county, state, and national campgrounds as well as camping shelters and cabins.

Campgrounds in Hawaii Volcanoes National Park are on a first-come, first-served basis. There are three drive-in campgrounds in the park. The one at Namakani Paio, 3.0 miles from the visitor center, and the one at Kipuka Nene, 11.5 miles from the visitor center, have water, shelters and cooking pits. The third campground, at Kamoamoa, at the southeast entrance to the park, offers spacious campsites with water, tables, shelters and fireplaces. Even in mid-summer, campsites are usually available at all campgrounds. There is a seven-day limit, but it is not strictly enforced. Campgrounds are free, but you must register at park headquarters to use the facilities and to secure a wilderness permit. I recommend Namakani Paio for a convenient and comfortable campground.

All other trail cabins and trail shelters are walk-in facilities. The two cabins on the trail to the summit of Mauna Loa—at Red Hill, 10,035 feet, and at the summit, 13,677 feet—are well-equipped with blankets, white-gas stoves, lanterns, heaters, and some cooking and eating utensils. You must supply Coleman fuel or white gas. Water is available, but should be treated with purifying tablets or boiled. The trail shelters at Kalue, Kipuka Pepeiau, Halape and Keauhou are simple overnight wilderness facilities with shelters, fireplaces and—usually—drinking water. Check with the ranger concerning water when you pick up your wilderness hiking permit. At Namakani Paio, the park concessionaire offers inexpensive cabins. These may be reserved by writing to Volcano House. (All addresses for writing to are in the appendix.)

Permits are required when camping at McKenzie State Park on the east coast, at Kalopa State Park on the northeast side and at Manuka State Park on the south side, the only state parks where camping is permitted. Of the three I recommend McKenzie because it is a beach park whereas Kalopa is in a wet area and it is not as conveniently located, and Manuka is just an overnight shelter. All the state parks are free, and they have water, shelter and fireplaces. Reservations are accepted and permits may be secured from the Division of State Parks. The state also operates three cabin facilities on the island that are comfortable and inexpensive. They are located at Mauna Kea State Park, at Hapuna Beach State Recreation Area, and at Kalopa State Recreation Area (see the camping map). Reservations and fee schedules may be obtained by writing to the state.

The County of Hawaii has established a system of beach parks which offer amenities from cold-water showers and drinking water to shelters, tables and firepits (see the camping map). Camping permits, required in these parks, may be secured in person or by writing to the County Department of Parks and Recreation. Permits may be obtained in person at Hale Halawai in Kailua-Kona (tel. 329-1989) or at the Yano Center, Captain Cook (tel. 323-3046). Camping fees at county parks are $1 per day, $.50 for persons 13-17.

The addresses of all these government agencies appear in the appendix.

Hiking

Hiking on the Big Island is an exciting and sometimes spectacular experience because of periodic volcanic activity. Few will dispute that the best trails and the most memorable experiences are to be found in Hawaii Volcanoes National Park. However, some prefer the North Kohala Mountains, with their verdant and precipitous valleys. For the backpacker who is looking for that "dream" unspoiled place, Waimanu provides an outstanding hiking experience, while the challenge of hiking to the two highest points in Hawaii—Mauna Kea and Mauna Loa—is irresistible. In any case, hiking on Hawaii does not generally require any special equipment or skill. Many places of unique and extraordinary beauty are readily accessible to the novice, to the family, and to the elderly who are looking for short, relatively easy hikes or walks. Although hiking boots are not essential on most hikes, I prefer them. I recommend strong shoes or hiking boots in the Hawaii Volcanoes National Park because of the rough lava surfaces. Most hikers find shorts or cutoffs adequate in areas up to 8000 feet. Even during the summer, however, warm clothing is necessary when hiking to the summit of Mauna Loa or Mauna Kea, both over 13,000 feet. Because snow and ice are not uncommon most of the year on both peaks, heavy sweaters and jackets are recommended. Hats and dark glasses are also necessary for protection from the weather and the glaring sun.

In 1975 the County of Hawaii began daily public transit service from Hilo to Kona and from Hilo to Hawaii Volcanoes National Park. Write the Hawaii County Transit System for more information and schedules. If bus transportation is available to the trailhead I have included routing instructions from Hilo and Kona after the driving instructions preceding introductory notes. Hitchhiking is presently legal, but rides are hard to get, especially in outlying areas.

1   Hawaii Volcanoes National Park

Rating: See individual hikes.

Features: Most active volcanoes in the world, national park from sea to summit (13,677 feet), wilderness camping, nene (rare Hawaiian state bird), camping, 22 hiking trails.

Permission: Written permits required for overnight hiking and camping in wilderness areas may be secured at the visitor center free in person or by mail (address the park superintendent). Camping is limited to 7 days per campground per year.

Hiking Distance and Time: See individual hikes.

Driving Instructions:
>From Hilo (30 miles, 1 hour) south on Route 11 to Park Entrance.
>From Kona (95 miles, 2+ hours) south on Route 11 to Park Entrance.

Bus Instructions:
>*From Hilo* Mooheau Terminal, Kamehameha Ave. downtown Hilo to Hawaii Volcanoes National Park.
>*From Kona* Kailua Post Office, Palani Rd. (opposite Kona Coast shopping center) to Mooheau Terminal in Hilo and transfer to Hawaii Volcanoes National Park.

Introductory Notes: Some visitors marvel at Kilauea's being a "drive-in volcano." Others are excited by being able to hike within the park from sea level to over 13,000 feet. Still others marvel at the fact that natural forces have added over 200 acres of land to the park since 1969. As recently as November 29, 1975, about 13 acres of land were lost as land settled into the sea in the Halape region of the park—the site of a wilderness camping area—as a result of a 7.2 magnitude earthquake and a tsunami (seismic sea wave). Yet it is typical of Hawaii that simultaneously about 28 acres of land were added as a result of seaward fault movements. The result was a net gain of 15 acres.

Change, change, and still more change is the attraction that draws hikers to the black-sand beaches and the lava-strewn slopes of Hawaii. It is the excitement, the anticipation that one can witness the elemental forces of nature at work close up and still survive. Of course, not everyone does survive. The toll of the November 1975 quake was one hiker killed and another still missing and presumed dead.

Hawaii Volcanoes National Park, established in 1916, includes Kilauea, the most active volcano in the world, and Mauna Loa volcano. Kilauea volcano is 4077 feet in elevation while the summit caldera of Mauna Loa presides at 13,677. The park's total land area is 344 square miles— at least that is what it was at the time of this writing. It is no exaggeration to note that this is subject to natural change.

For convenience, I have divided the park into four hiking areas. The division is somewhat natural, for each area has some unique characteristics. First, the Mauna Loa Strip Road area has the most difficult hike on the island—the 18.9-mile hike to the summit of Mauna Loa. Second, the Kilauea caldera area is the most popular hiking area. Most of the hikes here are short and easy, and perhaps the most exciting, for two trails cross the floors of active volcanoes. Third, the Kau Desert area is a hot, arid, somewhat barren area where hiking is strenuous and yet rewarding, for most of the trails cross recent lava flows, while others lead to the coastal wilderness areas of the park. Fourth, the Kalapana area is the area where, in 1969, Madame Pele erupted along a line of fissures southeast of the Kilauea caldera and buried three miles of the Chain of Craters Road, thus isolating the Kalapana section of the park. Subsequent eruptions cut off more of the road. In June 1979 a new Chain of Craters Road was opened, thus completing the so-called Golden Triangle, which enables a visitor to travel from Hilo to Hawaii Volcanoes National Park and back without doubling back on the same highway. Hiking trails in the Kalapana area take you to an ancient Hawaiian village and to some of the best examples of petroglyphs on the island.

In planning your hiking in the park, consult the Hiking Chart and the maps in this guide. The former will help you select hikes that fit your interests, time schedule, and physical condition. The maps will reveal connecting trails and combinations of trials to return to your starting point or to a convenient location for transportation.

Camping in the park is enjoyable for a couple of reasons. It's free whether you use the "civilized" campgrounds, the wilderness campgrounds or the cabins on Mauna Loa. These accommodations are also uncrowded and comfortable. Permits are necessary only to use the trail cabins and the wilderness campgrounds. See the area maps for the location of camping areas and the text for information about camping accommodations.

For safety, you MUST register with the park rangers at the visitor center for overnight hiking and for use of wilderness camping areas.

Because the hiking surface ranges from hard, crusted lava to soft volcanic ash and cinders, sound hiking boots are recommended for protection and comfort. A poncho is suggested in the Kilauea caldera area, which receives 95 inches of rain annually. Sun protection is a good idea in all other areas.

Mauna Loa Strip Road Area

The most notable trek in this hiking area is the climb to the summit of Mauna Loa. It is the most difficult and demanding hike on the island, due to the elevation gain. However, do not overlook the short, easy hike around Kipuka Puaula for an informative introduction to Hawaiian flora and fauna. The two hikes in this area begin at the Mauna Loa Strip Road, which begins about two miles west of the visitor center on Route 11. The strip road, though narrow, is paved and well maintained.

Mauna Loa summit, 18.9 miles one-way, 3-4 days (trail rating: difficult). Elevation gain 7015 feet.

The ascent of Mauna Loa should be attempted only after

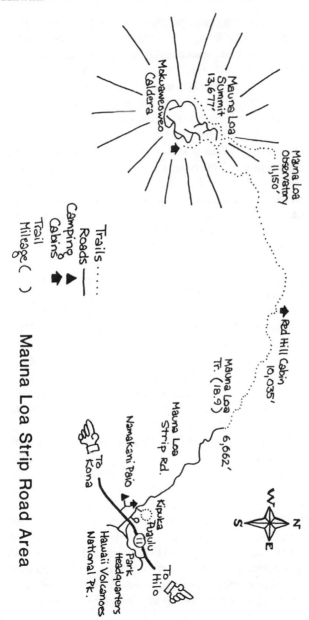

Mauna Loa Strip Road Area

Legend:
- Trails ......
- Roads ——
- Camping
- Cabins ▶
- Trail Mileage ( )

Map labels:
- Mokuaweoweo Caldera
- Mauna Loa Summit 13,677'
- Mauna Loa Observatory 11,150'
- Red Hill Cabin 10,035'
- Mauna Loa Tr. (18.9)
- 6,662'
- Mauna Loa Strip Rd.
- Namakani Paio
- Kipuka Puaulu
- To Kona
- To Hilo
- Park Headquarters
- Hawaii Volcanoes National Pk.

considerable planning and preparation. Bear in mind that even if you take 3 or 4 days, there is a considerable altitude change and mountain sickness is a possibility. Another consideration is hypothermia, which sets in when the body is not able to generate enough heat to keep the vital organs warm. Therefore, even during the summer, carry warm clothing including a heavy sweater or jacket and a warm sleeping bag protected from the rain by a plastic bag or water-repellent cover. The cabins at Red Hill and at the summit are no longer supplied. You must carry a cooking stove, fuel, eating utensils and, of course, food. The water at each cabin, collected from roof runoff, should be boiled or treated with purifying tablets. Both cabins are free, but you must sign up with the ranger at the visitor center for their use and for hiking permits (they must know who is where in case Pele causes a disturbance).

You should allow at least two days for the ascent: one day to hike to Red Hill (7.1 miles, 3373 feet gain), and another day to hike to the summit (11.8 miles, 3642 feet gain). You will probably find that 4 days are necessary for the round trip unless you are a good hiker in good condition.

On the Trail: The trailhead (6662 feet) is at the end of the Mauna Loa (lit., "Long Mountain") Strip Road some 13.5 miles from the Kilauea Visitor Center. There are a parking area and a picnic shelter at the road's end. You can hitchhike to this trailhead if you don't have a car.

The excitement of this hike begins immediately. The trailhead is a favorite habitat of the nene (*Branta sandvicensis*), the Hawaiian state bird. At the turn of this century, this native goose was close to extinction. In 1914, Herbert Shipman, a Hawaii Island rancher, began raising a pair. Later the National Park Service began a program to raise goslings and to return them to the wilds. Today, an estimated 1000 nenes are surviving on Hawaii and Maui. Natural breeding is difficult owing, in part, to a number of introduced predators, such as mongooses, pigs, and feral dogs and cats, for whom the eggs and the young goslings are easy prey. The nene has adapted to its rugged habitat on the rough lava flows far from any standing or running water, and some people suggest that this water fowl is more accurately regarded as a lava fowl. The most noticeable anatomical change has been the reduction of webbing between the toes, which better suits its terrestrial life. Its size (22-26″) and its variety of muted calls, often resembling the "moo" of a cow, make it easy to identify. If you spot a nene, don't be surprised if it walks up to you. They are very friendly birds and have been known to enjoy a petting!

The trail passes through a gate in a fence designed to protect the park from feral goats, whose voracious eating habits tend to denude the vegetation. Be sure to close the gate. Soon you are beyond nene country and above the open ohia (*Metrosideros collina*) forest at the 8300-foot level. The bright red blossom of the ohia lehua, the flower of the island of Hawaii, is regarded as sacred to Pele. Legend holds that if a person picks this flower on the way to the mountain, it will rain.

The Red Hill cabin at 10,035 feet is a welcome sight in what is now open country with little growth. It is a comfortable overnight facility and offers a panorama of the island. On a clear day you can see Maui to the northwest and its summit Haleakala—the house of the sun. If you are suffering from altitude sickness—a headache and a nauseous feeling—Red Hill is a good place to lie down with your head lower than your trunk and perhaps take an aspirin.

An early start on the second day will enable you to make a few miles before the hottest part of the day. Your hike to the summit follows the northeast rift of Mauna Loa, where you will find some startling cracks and shapes in the strata caused by recent splatter cones and lava flows. One eruption along this rift, in 1942, extended over a 2.8-mile area. The lava flowed to within 12 miles of the city of Hilo.

About two miles from the summit, you finally arrive at the North Pit of the great Mokuaweoweo (lit., "fish section"—red part of a fish, which suggests volcanic fires) caldera. The giant Mokuaweoweo caldera is an oval depression 3 miles long, 1½ miles wide, and as deep as 600 feet. The trail to the cabin drops into the caldera and crosses the smooth, flat surface, skirting to the right of Lua Poholo, a deep pit crater formed since 1841. The cabin is a short hike up to the rim of Mokuaweoweo. You'll find water at the cabin or ice in a lava crack, a short (½ mile) walk southwest of the cabin.

To reach the summit you must return to the junction on the north side of the caldera and follow the ahus (rock cairns) to the 13,677-foot summit. At the summit you are standing on the top of the world's largest active shield volcano and the largest single mountain on earth, when you consider that it rises about 30,000 feet above its base on the ocean floor.

Mauna Loa has been surprisingly quiet for over 20 years. The last eruption from Mokuaweoweo caldera was in 1949, when more than half the caldera floor was blanketed with new lava. The eruption of Mauna Loa in 1950, the greatest since 1859, was along the southwest rift, with fissures from 11,000 feet down to 8000 feet. Lava flowed westward and southeastward, and within a day had reached the sea. When lava entered the water, it boiled, and steam clouds rose 10,000 feet into the air. An estimated billion tons of lava destroyed two dozen buildings and buried a mile of highway. No lives were lost.

The return trip to the trailhead is easy, but tiring if you do it in one day. An alternate return is to take the observatory trail. From the summit, return along the trail for 1.6 miles to a spur trail that goes northwest (left) for 0.3 mile to the emergency four-wheel drive road and the Observatory Trail. The trail is on the left side of the road, extending 3 steep and difficult miles to the Mauna Loa weather observatory at 11,150 feet while the road switchbacks to the observatory. Unless you have made arrangements for someone to drive to the observatory to pick you up, it is 19 miles from the observatory to Route #20, and 28 miles on Route #20 to Hilo.

Kilauea Caldera Area

Without question, the Kilauea (lit., "spewing"— referring to eruptions) section of the national park is the most exciting place on the island because dramatic change is always imminent. Like Mauna Loa, Kilauea is a shield volcano with a characteristic broad, gently sloping dome. While the summit is 4000 feet above sea level, the base of the mountain extends another 16,000 feet to the ocean bottom. The summit caldera, 2½ miles long and 2 miles wide, contains Halemaumau, the "fire pit," which is the legendary home of Pele, the goddess of volcanoes. Halemaumau had an almost continuously active lake of liquid lava through the 19th century and the first quarter of the 20th. One commentator in 1826 noted that "the bottom was covered with lava, and the southwest and northern parts of it were one vast flood of burning matter, in a terrific state of ebullition, rolling to and fro its 'fiery surge' and flaming billows..." Today, Kilauea is not as active or quite as romantic, but it continues to provide visitors with some exciting moments and thrilling experiences.

The Kilauea portion of the park is the most popular hiking area on the island because of the presence of active Kilauea and because of easy access to hiking trails. In planning your hiking, consult the maps and the text for connecting trails, since most of the trails do not loop. For example, one hike that I would recommend is to take the Halemaumau Trail across the caldera to the "fire pit," connect with the Byron Ledge Trail to the Kilauea Iki Trail, which ends at the Thurston Lava Tube, and then return to the visitor center via the Crater Rim Trail. This is approximately a 10-mile loop. No special equipment is necessary. However, I recommend a strong, durable pair of boots or shoes, water, sun protection and food.

Crater Rim Trail, 11.6 mile loop, 1 day (trail rating: strenuous).

The best introduction to the Kilauea area is to drive the Crater Rim Road or to hike the Crater Rim Trail, which circles the caldera. It is a strenuous hike with 500

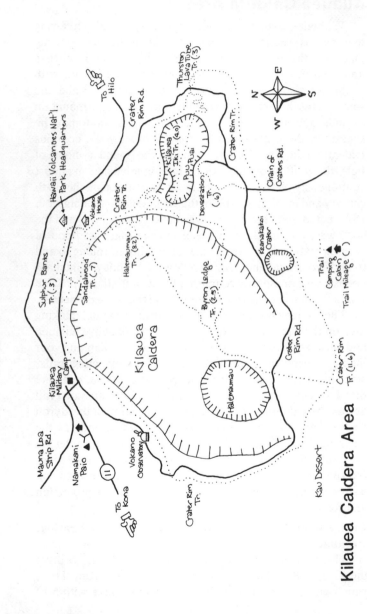

Kilauea Caldera Area

See Hawaii as few have –

HAWAIIAN OUTDOOR ADVENTURES

WITH

**HIKING
SWIMMING
SNORKELING
SURFING
FISHING
SHELLING
BEACHCOMBING**

Robert Smith, Author and Outdoorsman

HAWAIIAN OUTDOOR ADVENTURES

17741 Misty Lane
Huntington Beach
California 92649
(714) 840-5888

(WRITE/CALL FOR FREE BROCHURE)

feet elevation gain. Plan on a full day to complete the hike. You will want to make some side trips to take in some of the sights and to pause frequently to enjoy the striking panoramas of the volcanic landscape.

On the Trail: Pick up the trail in front of the Volcano House, turn right, and hike the loop counterclockwise in order to pass through the warm Kau Desert before noon. The trail initially passes a few steaming vents, which seem to set the mood. At "Steaming Bluff" billowing steam clouds rise from the ground, caused by water getting into the "plumbing" of Kilauea. The steam is accompanied by small amounts of hydrogen sulfide, which smells like rotten eggs. This condition is an eerie introduction to your hike.

The trail continues along the crater rim, passes the Kilauea Military Camp on the opposite side of the road, and climbs slightly up Uwekahuna (lit., "wailing priest") Bluff to the site of the Hawaii Volcano Observatory. From here, scientists have been keeping a watchful eye on Kilauea since 1911, when Dr. Thomas A. Jaggar established the observatory. Today, studies continue under the direction of the U.S. Geological Survey. Pause to examine the seismograph that monitors earth movements in the area. It is also a good place from which to view Halemaumau and Kilauea and, on a clear day, to admire the striking presence of towering Mauna Loa to the west. This, the highest point on the trail, was once a sacred point for Hawaiians, where offerings were made to the gods.

From the observatory, the trail dips south along the road and then crosses it to the southwest rift of Kilauea and to the trailhead for the Kau Desert region. It was along the southwest rift that an eruption occurred in 1971 which lasted five days and covered an area of 1.3 square miles. (A rift is a highly fractured land area on the flank of a volcano along which most of the volcano's eruptions take place.)

You might choose to take the Halemaumau Trail to the "fire pit." The fire pit is about a mile off the rim trail across the Crater Rim Road to the east side of the caldera (see the

Halemaumau Trail below). If not, you may smell the sulfur fumes being emitted by Halemaumau.

The Keanakakoi (lit., "cave of the adzes") Crater marks the beginning of the east rift zone, where in 1974 one of the last major eruptions of Kilauea occurred. During the first part of that year, the Kilauea caldera began to swell, and earthquake activity increased. Finally, in July, rifts opened on the southeastern caldera rim and in the caldera floor, while 200-foot fountains of incandescent lava spurted from fissures. Lava filled Keanakakoi Crater and flowed beyond to cover the Chain of Craters Road.

From here to the fern forest you should find many ohelo (*Vaccinium reticulatum*) shrubs bearing delectable bright red berries. A small native shrub in the cranberry family, it has many branches with small, rounded, toothed leaves. The berries are edible but sacred to Pele. To avoid Pele's wrath, you should throw half your berries into the fire pit saying,

> *E Pele, here are your ohelos.*
> *I offer some to you.*
> *Some I also eat.*

After crossing the Chain of Craters Road, the trail passes through a sparsely wooded area before entering a thick tree-fern forest. Here you will find some outstanding specimens of Hawaiian tree ferns. The hapuu (*Cibotium splendens*) is an endemic fern that can reach 16 feet in height. In old Hawaii, hats were made from the stems. The starchy trunk core was used for cooking and for washing. Another endemic tree fern is the amaumau (*Sadleria splendens*), from which the fire pit Halemaumau (lit. "house of ferns") derives its name. The fronds were used for thatching house frames and for making red dye to color tapa cloth. Ample rain—about 95 inches annually—sustains this verdant and enchanting forest. The forest is shaded by a canopy of ohia lehua (*Metrosideros collina*) trees with red powder-puff-like blossoms, which were regarded as sacred to Pele. Hawaiians believed that it would rain if the flower was picked.

The Thurston Lava Tube Trail is a short spur trail off the

Crater Rim Trail; it takes you through a 450-foot lava tunnel (see Thurston Lava Tube Trail description).

Pick up the Crater Rim Trail by crossing the road and parking lot from the lava tube. The trail follows the edge of Kilauea Iki crater, a pit crater immediately adjacent to the eastern edge of Kilauea caldera. The trail is shaded and cool and offers a number of lookout points with interpretive exhibit cases.

The trail and the road along Waldron Ledge were closed after the November 1975 earthquake when some of the ledge fell into the crater and much of the road was severely fractured. The trail has since been repaired, and it is safe to proceed with caution and to view the power of nature first-hand. A short walk from here will return you to Volcano House.

Halemaumau Trail, 3.2 miles one-way, 2 hours (trail rating: hardy family).

As you approach the trail across the lava lake floor of the Kilauea caldera, you may be apprehensive. Knowing that the earth is boiling below your every step can be overwhelming. Consequently, while the hiking is irresistible, you can't wait to finish the hike and get out of the caldera.

If your starting point is Volcano House, you might plan a loop trip (consult maps) or arrange to be picked up on the opposite side unless you plan to return across the crater.

On the Trail: To reach the Halemaumau Trail from Volcano House, follow the footpath in front of Volcano House (facing Kilauea) to the right until it joins the Sandalwood Trail. Go left on the Sandalwood Trail a short distance, and then left on the Halemaumau Trail, which drops about 500 feet to the floor of the caldera.

The hike across the caldera is hot and dry, so sun protection and water are important. As you approach the rough, brittle, twisted, broken surface, an eerie, somewhat uncomfortable feeling sets in, so that as a piece of rock crumbles underfoot, you swallow hard and breathe a bit more deeply for a moment. The trail is well marked with ahus (rock cairns) and is easy to follow. The shiny black surface of the pahoehoe (smooth and ropy surface) lava sometimes nearly blinds you. The first half mile is fresh lava from a 1974 flow. In fact the trail crosses lava dating from 1885, 1954, 1971 and 1975. See if you can notice the difference.

The caldera has literally had its ups and downs over the years as it has been filled and emptied by successive eruptions. The depth of the caldera changes with almost every eruption as the floor swells and erupts. Some craters fill up and others shrink.

Beyond the junction with the Byron Ledge Trail, the Park Service has constructed a safe viewing overlook into Halemaumau, the "fire pit" and the home of the goddess Pele. Typically, there are steam clouds and an unpleasant "rotten egg" odor. From here you can view the panorama from left to right, beginning with the summit of Mauna Loa, then the crater rim with the Volcano Observatory, the Steaming Bluffs, Volcano House and Byron Ledge, dividing Kilauea from Kilauea Iki.

The trail continues across the Crater Rim Road to connect with the Crater Rim Trail. However, you may choose to return via the Byron Ledge Trail or the Rim Road.

Byron Ledge Trail, 2.5 miles one-way, 1½ hours (trail rating: strenuous).

This is a convenient trail to connect with other trails or to return to park headquarters after hiking the Halemaumau Trail.

On the Trail: From the fire pit (Halemaumau), the trail crosses Kilauea caldera eastward and climbs a few hundred feet to Byron Ledge, which separates Kilauea from Kilauea Iki. From the bluff you have views of both craters and of Puu Puai (lit., "gushing hill"), a 400-foot cone of pumice and ash on the south side of Kilauea Iki formed by an eruption in 1959. After the November 1975 earthquake, the ledge trail was closed due to slides on the west wall of Kilauea Iki. In the Summer of 1976 Park Service trail crews re-routed the trail, enabling you to hike once again into Kilauea Iki.

Kilauea Iki Trail, 2.0 miles, 1½ hours one way (trail rating: strenuous).

On the Trail: The Kilauea Iki (lit., "little Kilauea") Trail is accessible from Thurston Lava Tube or from Volcano House via the Halemaumau, Byron Ledge, or Crater Rim Trail. From Byron Ledge or Crater Rim, the trail descends 400 feet into the crater. This newly constructed trail was built after slides covered the old trail following the earthquake of November 1975. The trail bisects the crater floor, which is covered with fresh lava from a spectacular 1959 eruption. This eruption, which lasted 36 days, had exploding fountains that reached a record-setting 1,900 feet in height. Cinder, pumice and ash piled up on the crater rim over five feet thick. The devastated area (see Devastation Trail description) south of the crater was created at this time, while a pool of lava 380 feet deep remained in the crater. Since then, scientists have been drilling core samples in an effort to study the cooling of lava. You will find a number of their drilling sites. Obviously these should be left undisturbed.

After the trail snakes about 400 feet up the western wall of the crater through an ohia tree-fern forest, it ends in the parking lot at Thurston Lava Tube.

Thurston Lava Tube Trail, .3-mile loop, 15 minutes (trail rating: family).

This is a short but a "must" trail in the Kilauea section. You can drive to the trail via the Crater Rim Road or hike the crater rim clockwise from Volcano House or from the western end of the Kilauea Iki Trail. This prehistoric lava tube was formed when the surface of a tongue of flowing lava cooled and solidified while the inner part continued to flow and eventually emptied the tube, leaving a 450-foot tunnel as high as 20 feet in places.

On the Trail: The trail to the tube entrance descends through a lush tree-fern forest. Many of the plants are identified by marker. Native birds are commonly found here. With luck you may see the small (4½") green and yellow amakihi (*Loxops virents*) foraging for food, or the vermillion i'iwi (*Vestiaria* *coccinea*) with black wings and a long, curved, salmon-colored bill and orange legs.

Devastation Trail, .6 mile one-way, 15 minutes (trail rating: family).

One of the most photographed and most popular areas in the park, the devastation area was created by a 1959 eruption in Kilauea Iki when 1,900-foot fountains showered the area with ash, pumice and spatter that buried an ohia forest, denuded ohia trees and left their skeletons standing in tribute to the eerie, strangely beautiful effects of Mother Nature. A boardwalk crosses the area to prevent passing feet from creating numerous trails.

You can drive to the trailhead from the Crater Rim Road or hike there via the Crater Rim Trail. It is a one-mile hike from the Thurston Lava Tube. Don't miss the Devastation Trail. It's weird!

Sandalwood Trail, .7 mile one-way, 15 minutes (trail rating: family).

The Sandalwood Trail is one of a number of short, easy trails from the visitor center to scenic overlooks of the Kilauea caldera. The trail begins west of Volcano House and gently descends for a hike along the caldera rim to the steam vents at Steaming Bluff. You pass through a rather dense ohia tree-fern forest where many of the plants are identified by marker. A number of steam vents along the trail remind you of the presence of Pele and send off the "rotten egg" smell caused by hydrogen sulfide. You can return to park headquarters via the Crater Rim Trail or the Sulfur Bank Trail.

Sulfur Bank Trail, .3 mile one-way, 15 minutes (trail rating: family).

An interesting trail from the visitor center will take you to the sulfur banks, where volcanic fumaroles emit gases that deposit colorful minerals. This is an easy walk and an interesting sight, but the presence of that "rotten egg" smell means you won't linger very long.

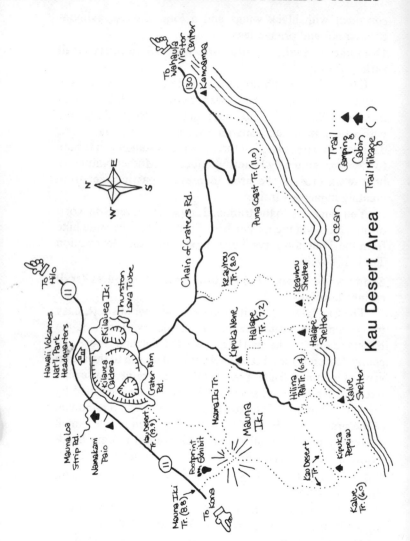

Kau Desert Area

The Kau Desert is indeed just that—a hot, arid, dry, relatively barren and bleak area that composes the southern section of Hawaii Volcanoes National Park. There are no precise boundaries, but the desert region is considered to be all the land south of Kilauea caldera between Route 11 in the west and the Chain of Craters Road in the east. All the trails here are long and hot, without any guarantee of water. It is an area that tests the hiker and his/her equipment, and perhaps appeals most to those who are seeking solitude. Compared to the other areas of the park, there are no sights to speak of— just a lot of lava, a lot of sun, a lot of stillness, and a lot of sweat!

Water is generally available at the trail cabin at Kipuka Pepeiau and at the trail shelters at Kipuka Nene, Kalue, Halape and Keauhou. However, check with a ranger at the visitor center for confirmation when you pick up your wilderness permit. Remember, the most striking character-istic of the park is change. For example, new shelters constructed at Halape in 1975 were destroyed a few months later by the November 1975 tsunami. Since then, a new shelter has been built and hundreds of coconut trees have been planted there.

Halape Trail, 7.2 miles one-way, 6 hours (trail rating: difficult). Elevation loss 3000 feet.

The most popular trail in the Kau Desert is the Halape Trail from the campground at Kipuka Nene (lit., "goose leap") to the coastal trail shelter at Halape. The well-defined trail descends through the Kau Desert about 3000 feet to the sea. The trailhead is at Kipuka Nene Campground, a 10½-mile drive over the Chain of Craters Road and the Hilina Pali Road from the visitor center. From the shelter, the trail crisscrosses a jeep road for a couple of miles and passes through low shrubs and grassland. From a junction with the Hilina Pali Trail, it is less that two miles to Halape. Once the allure at Halape was the oasislike character of hundreds of coconut trees bordering a peaceful lagoon. However, on the morning of November 29, 1975, this was all changed when the island was hit by an earthquake that registered a high 7.2 on the Richter scale at the Hawaii Volcano Observatory. Roads and trails in the park were severely damaged, and at Halape a tsunami (seismic sea wave) battered the shore. It was the largest ever recorded in Hawaii, cresting at 30 feet and traveling at a staggering 187 miles per hour. Simultaneously, the land sank about six feet, an event that experts say reduced the impact of the tsunami. However, to the 32 campers at Halape, it was a nightmare, as successive waves picked up people, horses, boulders, trees and camping equipment and created a swirling mass. One camper found himself floating out to sea on the roof of the trail shelter before he jumped off and luckily swam to safety. Others were thrown into cracks in the earth, while still others clung to trees, shrubs and rocks and, thereby, to life. Miraculously, all but two campers survived. Today, calm has returned to Halape, where a new sandy beach and a cave have been formed. The Park Service worked through the summer of 1976 repairing the trail and the shelter at Halape and planting new coconut trees to replace those that were under six feet of water in June 1976.

Hilina Pali Trail, 6.4 miles one-way to Halape Trail Junction, 4 hours (trail rating: strenuous). Elevation loss 2000 feet.

The Hilina Pali (lit., "struck cliff") Trail begins at the end of the Hilina Pali Road (15 miles from the visitor center). From the trailhead, the Kau Desert Trail goes southwest (4.8 miles) to the cabin at Kipuka Pepeiau while the Hilina Pali Trail descends the pali southeast to connect with the Halape Trail some 6.4 miles distant. It is a hot, arid hike with water available at Kipuka Pepeiau and Halape (but confirm this with a ranger first). Our trail's name is derived from the Hilina Pali Fault, a dramatic example of faulting. A fault is created when a fracture occurs in the earth's crust and the block on one side moves with respect to the block on the other side. During the earthquake of November 1975, the south flank of Kilauea slumped seaward along the 15-mile Hilina Pali Fault to produce major effects.

On the Trail: The trail southeast from the Hilina Pali Road descends about 2300 feet to the coast, to the Halape Shelter via the Halape Trail or to the Kalue Shelter via the Kalue

Trail. The descent of the pali is a little treacherous, but with some caution it can be negotiated safely. After 2.2 miles the trail reaches a junction with the Kalue Trail, which goes south 1.6 miles to the Kalue Shelter on the coast. At another junction 1.2 miles beyond, the Hilina Pali Trail meets a trail that goes southwest 1.6 miles to the Kalue Shelter. From this junction the Hilina Pali Trail goes 3.0 miles northeast to join the Halape Trail, on which you can head south to Halape or north to Kipuka Nene.

Kau Desert Trail 19.9 miles one-way one day (trail rating: difficult). Elevation loss 4000 feet.

To traverse the entire length of the Kau Desert Trail from the west side of the Kilauea caldera off the Crater Rim Trail to the trail cabin at Kipuka Pepeiau and to the Hilina Pali Road requires a stout heart, strong legs and water. This is a long, arid trail that drops about 2000 feet. If you have the time (three days minimum) and are seeking solitude, a vigorous hike can be made by taking the Kau Desert Trail to the end of the Hilina Pali Road, taking the Hilina Pali Trail to Halape, and returning via the Halape Trail to Kipuka Nene (35.1 miles).

On the Trail: The trail gradually descends through some low scrub vegetation and then across relatively barren pahoehoe lava. Look in the pukas (holes) for "Pele's hair," a thin, golden substance consisting of volcanic glass spun into hair-like strands. It is plentiful on this older lava form, as is Hawaiian "snow," a whitish lichen that is the first thing to grow on new lava. From the trail junction with the Mauna Iki Trail, an easy, gradual climb to the summit of Mauna Iki (3032 feet) provides interesting panoramas of the surrounding area. From the summit you can take the Mauna Iki Trail west to the "footprints" exhibit (see the Mauna Iki Trail for their description). The trail to Kipuka Pepeiau is an easy descent skirting the Kamakaia (lit., "the fish eye") Hills to Kipuka Pepeiau.

From the cabin, the Kau Desert trail parallels a fault system as it leads to the Hilina Pali Road and Overlook.

There are a number of interesting cracks in the earth along the trail which permit you to study a fault system up close. Notice the scars and tears in the pali (cliff) walls where the earth has slipped and has been torn away. From the pali there are dramatic views of the Kau Desert and the coast.

Mauna Iki Trail, 8.8 miles one-way, 8 hours (trail rating: strenuous).

Crossing the Kau Desert east-west, the Mauna Iki (lit., "little mountain") Trail connects the Hilina Pali Road and Route 11, and bisects the Kau Desert Trail. This convenient trail enables the visitor to cut hiking distance and time to points of interest in the desert.

On the Trail: If you begin your hike at Route 11 (9.1 miles from the visitor center) you can conveniently visit the footprints exhibit. There is a highway sign noting the trailhead. From here, it is an easy .8-mile hike to the footprints over a broad, well-defined trail. Some of the footprints are in protected enclosures to prevent vandalism and to shelter them from the elements. It is here that armies assembled in 1790 to prepare for battle for control of the island. The armies opposing Kamehameha the Great were overcome by the fumes and dust from Halemaumau, and their footprints were left in the hardening ash. Some believe that Pele interceded to assist Kamehameha. If you search the area, you can find other footprints, although those under glass are the most distinguishable.

The trail continues to the top of Mauna Iki (3032 feet) and to a junction with the Kau Desert Trail. The trail is well defined by rock cairns. Some of the lava is from the recent flows of 1971. Indeed, Mauna Iki is geologically an infant, having been formed in 1920. It is a satellite shield volcano, built by lava flows from Halemaumau. There are countless cracks in the area that are part of the southwest rift of Kilauea. It is a fascinating place to investigate, but do so with caution.

From Mauna Iki follow the Kau Desert Trail north .7 mile to a continuation of the Mauna Iki Trail, which traverses the desert to the Hilina Pali Road. Along this trail you can find handfuls of "Pele's hair": thin, golden, spun volcanic glass in hairlike strands. It is also a good chance to examine and to photograph outstanding examples of pahoehoe feet and toes where the lava has naturally flowed to form footlike shapes. Additionally, you will find lava rivers, numerous pit craters and small cinder cones.

As you approach a low scrub area, the trail is not distinguishable, but if you continue due east you can't miss the road and your trail's end. From here, it is about 1 mile south to the campground at Kipuka Nene, 4 miles north to the Chain of Craters Road and 10½ miles to the visitor center.

Kalapana Area

The forces of nature isolated the southern section of the Hawaii Volcanoes National Park between 1969 and 1979. Beginning in 1969 a series of eruptions from Kilauea covered miles of the road connecting the Kilauea Visitor Center with the Kalapana area. For 10 years it was a 55-mile drive from the Kilauea center to the Wahaula Visitor Center on Route 130. Today, it is a scenic and pleasant ride of 28 miles from the Kilauea to the Wahaula visitor area. Two hikes enable a person to see three relatively new craters and examine some outstanding petroglyphs.

Puu Loa Petroglyphs, 1 mile one-way, 3/4 hour (trail rating: hardy family).

The trailhead is marked by a road sign 8.5 miles west of the Wahaula Visitor Center. The trail to the Puu Loa (lit., "long hill") Petroglyphs is marked and well-worn as it crosses pahoehoe lava, which has a smooth and ropy surface, unlike aa lava, which has a rough, clinkery surface. The view up-country from the trail offers a panorama of the Kilauea eruptions of 1969 through 1972, which flowed to the sea and covered much of the Chain of Craters Road.

You will find the petroglyphs on mounds. There are hundreds, in varying sizes and shapes. There are dots,

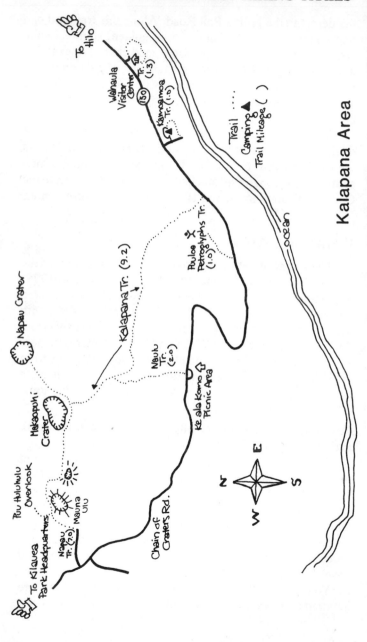

Kalapana Area

dashes, lines and bars as well as some figures that are somewhat distinguishable. Holes in the lava (pukas) were receptacles in which ancient Hawaiians placed the umbilical cords of their children, supposedly to insure a long life.

Naulu Trail, 2 miles one-way, 1 hour (trail rating: hardy family).

The Naulu (lit., "the groves") trailhead is located on the north side of the Chain of Craters Road 13.6 miles from the Kilauea Visitor Center and 14.4 miles from the Wahaula Visitor Center. Until the lava flows of 1972 Naulu was a popular forest and picnic area. Today, the trail is useful because it provides convenient access to the Kalapana Trail, which in turn provides access to a number of interesting craters.

On the Trail: The trail begins opposite a turnout along the Chain of Craters Road, Ke Ala Komo (lit., "entrance path"), where there was once a populous village. The first 0.2 mile of the trail, over rough aa lava, parallels the road until it emerges on a 1971 pahoehoe lava flow from Mauna Ulu. Since Naulu is a newly established trail, the lava is not worn, so it is necessary to follow the ahus, or stone piles, as you make your way north. There is no shelter or shade from the hot sun, nor any water. On the right and front right, numerous trees and a variety of scrub have survived successive lava flows. After the first mile the summit of Mauna Ulu comes into view on the left. Near the end of the trail you reach the remains of the old Chain of Craters Road. Follow the road northwest (left) for a short distance to a junction with the Kalapana Trail. From here you can take the Kalapana Trail east 8 miles to the coastline or northwest 1.2 miles to join the Napau Trail.

Napau Trail, 7 miles one-way, 4 hour (trail rating: strenuous).

The Napau (lit., "the endings") area provides an opportunity to observe recent lava flows, volcanic craters, and stages in the growth of a shield volcano. To reach the trailhead drive the Chain of Craters Road toward the coast and make a left turn at a sign, "Mauna Ulu." Drive a short distance to the end of the road and a trailhead marker.

On the Trail: The first part of the trail traverses the gently sloping flanks of Puu Huluhulu (lit., "shaggy hill"), a prehistoric cinder and spatter cone which stands northwest of a newly built shield volcano, Mauna Ulu (lit., "growing mountain"). Major eruptions broke out along the east rift of Kilauea in 1969, with fountains spewing forth along a fissure that paralleled the Chain of Craters Road. By June 1969 repeated flows and the accumulation of spatter and cinder had built a gently sloping, shield-shaped cone more than a mile across and 400 feet high. Thus was Mauna Ulu born. Subsequent flows filled some nearby craters and covered parts of the road. At a junction one mile from the trailhead, a short trail on he left (north) leads to the Puu Huluhulu overlook.

Some startling shapes formed by the pahoehoe (smooth and ropy surface) lava are found along the entire length of the trail. Search the pukas (holes) in the lava for "Pele's hair," a golden, hairlike substance consisting of volcanic glass spun in gossamer form.

Beyond Mauna Ulu the trail passes north of Alae (lit., "mudhen"), a pit crater created in 1969. In that year, successive eruptions and lava flows from both Alae and Mauna Ulu alternately filled and emptied Alae Crater. It's an exciting and interesting spot.

From near Alae the trail gently descends about 3 miles to a junction with the Kalapana Trail near Makaopuhi (lit., "eye of eel") Crater, which is a crater second in size to Kilauea. Recent eruptions (1965, 1969) from fissures on the flanks of Makaopuhi (part of the east rift zone of Kilauea) have created havoc and change; the most notable was the destruction of the Chain of Craters Road. From the Napau/Makaopuhi junction, it is two miles to Napau Crater. Not unlike its neighbors, Napau has been active in recent years. Its most dramatic contribution came in 1965 when lava from the crater created a forest of tree molds.

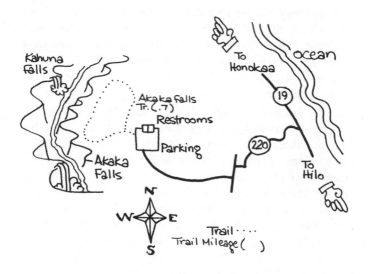

2   Akaka Falls

Rating: Family.

Features: 420-foot Akaka Falls, Kahuna Falls, native and introduced flora.

Permission: None.

Hiking Distance and Time: .7 mile loop, ½ hour.

Driving Instructions:

From Hilo (15 miles, 3/4 hour) north on Route 19, left on Route 220 to end.

From Kona (87 miles, 2½ hours) north on Route 190, right on Route 220 to end.

Bus Instruction:

From Hilo Mooheau Terminal, Kamehameha Ave. downtown to Honomu. Walk or hitchhike (3.9 miles) west on Route 220 to Akaka Falls State Park.

From Kona Kailua Post Office, Palani Rd. (opposite Kona Coast shopping center) to Honomu, then as above.

Introductory Notes: Few dispute that Akaka (lit., "clearness") Falls State Park is everyone's idea of what Hawaii is all about. It is a 66-acre tropical paradise in a canyon park where all of nature's riches seem larger than life. Everything—the ti, the ginger, the bamboo, the tree ferns, the orchids, the azaleas—comes in the large economy size!

On the Trail: A paved trail descends abruptly from the parking lot and thrusts the hiker immediately into the canyon, where a large variety of tropical plants greet one. A guide to Hawaiian flora, such as the one by Dorothy and Bob Hargreaves (*Hawaiian Blossoms*) is handy to help you identify the many varieties of plants.

Giant bamboo on the right dominates the first part of the trail. Bamboo has long been an important product on the islands, having been used for fuel, furniture, buildings, musical instruments, utensils and paper. Indeed, bamboo sprouts are commonly eaten as a vegetable on the islands.

Your nose will identify the delicately fragrant yellow ginger (*Zingiber zerumbet*) before you see it. It has a light-yellow blossom that rises at the end of narrow tube with olive-colored bracts. The leaves are a luxuriant green. You will also find giant torch ginger, red ginger and shell ginger, with its shell-like flowers. And there's more: banana, plumeria, ti, ohia lehua, a variety of hibiscus (the Hawaii state flower), bird of paradise, heliconia and azalea, to cite a partial list.

At about midpoint on the trail an overlook offers a spectacular view of Kahuna (lit., "the hidden one") Falls on the north side of the canyon. Farther up the canyon, however, is the showpiece of the park. Towering, 420-foot Akaka Falls slips over a ridge and falls lazily into Kolekole (lit., "raw, scarred") Stream, where it nourishes nature's lush gardens. Seeing it is a breathless moment in an exciting forest.

Waipio/Waimanu Valleys

Rating: Difficult. Elevation gain and loss 1000 feet.

Features: Ancient Hawaiian settlement, abandoned Peace Corps training area, native and introduced flora and fauna, wilderness camping, mountain apple, rose apple.

Permission: Call Theo Davies Hamakua Sugar Co. for camping permit in Waipio Valley (776-1211).

Hiking Distance & Time: 9 miles one-way, 7 hours.

Driving Instructions:

From Hilo (50 miles, 1½ hours) north on Route 19, right on Route 240, to end of road at Waipio Lookout.

From Kona (65 miles, 2 hours) north on Route 190, right on Route 19, left on Route 240 to end of road at Waipio Lookout.

Bus Instructions:

From Hilo Mooheau Terminal, Kamehameha Ave. downtown to Honokaa. Walk or hitchhike (9.1 miles) northwest to Waipio Lookout.

From Kona Kailua Post Office, Palani Rd. (opposite Kona Coast shopping center) to Honokaa, then as above.

Introductory Notes: When outdoorsmen talk about hiking in Hawaii, they talk about the Kalalau Trail on Kauai, Kipahulu Valley on Maui, and Waipio and Waimanu on the Big Island. These are the ultimate in wilderness experiences in Hawaii.

Historically, Waipio and Waimanu Valleys were important centers of Hawaiian civilization, particularly Waipio (lit., "curved water"), the larger of the two. Fertile soil and ample water reportedly sustained as many as 50,000 people before the white man arrived. In the past, sugar cane, taro and bananas carpeted this six-mile valley.

In 1823 the first white men visited Waipio and found a thriving community. They were told that Waipio was once a favorite place of Hawaiian royalty; indeed, in 1780,

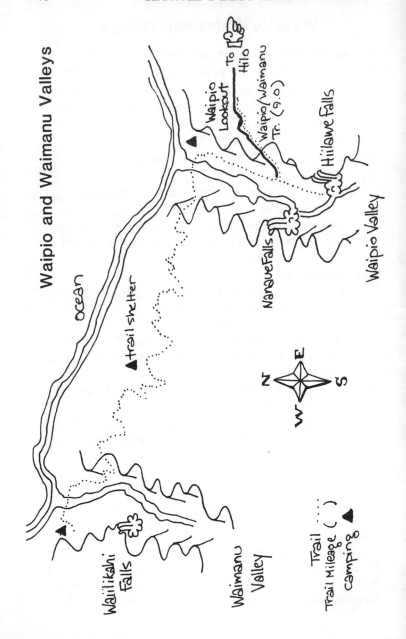

Waipio and Waimanu Valleys

To Hilo

Waipio Lookout

Waipio/Waimanu Tr. (9.0)

Hiilawe Falls

Nanaue Falls

Waipio Valley

ocean

trail shelter

N E W S

Wailikahi Falls

Waimanu Valley

Trail

Trail Mileage ( )

Camping

Kamehameha is reported to have received there his war god, who singled him out as the future ruler of the islands. Later, Chinese immigrants came to Waipio, where they cultivated rice until the 1930's.

Today Waipio's population has declined to a few dozen, but taro continues to be an important crop. Most of the farmers now live in towns on the plateau east of the valley, where electricity and other amenities are more readily available. Periodic tsunamis—tidal waves—have also discouraged permanent settlement. However, some people are returning to their ancestral homes upon retirement.

Guided tours of the valley are available in four-wheel-drive vehicles. (It is impossible for a conventional car to negotiate the 26%-grade jeep road into the valley.) Arrangements can be made at the lookout when you arrive.

Waimanu (lit., "bird water") Valley is not as deep or as wide as Waipio. Nevertheless, this verdant valley once sustained a sizable population, as evidenced by the stone walls and terraces that remain.

On the Trail: The trailhead is at the pavilion overlooking Waipio Valley, a 900-foot-high perch with a striking panorama. Your eye can easily follow the trail leading to Waimanu, which snakes up the northwest wall of Waipio Valley. Numerous waterfalls drop into Waipio from the Kohala Mountains.

Carry as much water as you can, since the only safe drinking water is at the bases of the waterfalls. Treat or boil other water. Water in the valley irrigates farms and serves cattle which graze in the Kohala Mountains.

The paved jeep-road trail drops an abrupt mile into Waipio Valley to a junction from where one road leads toward the beach and the other into the valley. Look for guava (*Psidium guajava*) on both sides of the road. The yellow, lemon-sized fruit is a tasty treat. The beach trail passes some homesteads along Lalakea (a kind of shark) Fishpond on its way to the gray sand beach. It is common to find locals pushing and dragging their outriggers on Waipio

Stream to the open sea for a day of fishing. Note how they use the undulations of the surf to carry them over the rock-laden outlet, and conversely to beach their craft. The thick, silky, green leaves of beach naupaka (*Scaevola frutescens*) greet the hiker on the beach. A common sight on most of Hawaii's beaches, the naupaka is a native variety that may grow to a height of ten feet. It has a small, fragrant, white flower with small white berries following the flowers.

Camping in Waipio Valley is allowed on the east side of Waipio Stream by securing permission from the Davies Hamakua Sugar Co. Until 1977 the best and most popular campsites were on the west side of the stream among the trees that front the beach, on property owned by the Bishop Museum of Honolulu. They closed the area to camping due to overcrowding. They have said they may allow camping in the future by permit only, limiting the number of campers.

Ford Waipio Stream where it enters the ocean and scout the beach for a picnic spot. The ironwood (*Casuarina equisetifolia*) trees that front the beach provide an umbrella from the hot sun and the rain. Also known at the Australian Pine, the ironwood has long, thin, drooping, dull-green needles whose droppings make a soft mat for a sleeping bag but are a fire danger. Approach ocean swimming with extreme caution: there is a strong surf with riptides.

There are a number of ways to explore Waipio. You can take the jeep road from the beach into the valley or follow the footpaths that surround the taro fields. This latter course is very wet and sometimes impassable where fences and *kapu* (keep out) signs block the way.

If you follow the jeep road into the valley, you can hike to some of Waipio's interesting places. Stay on the left along the base of the cliff, and the road will take you to a pavilion on the hillside below Hiilawe (lit., "lift [and]-carry") Falls. The falls may not be "turned on," since the stream that feeds it is used for irrigation and the water is frequently taken out above the falls. The building here was intended to be a restaurant, but is instead used by the Bishop Museum of Honolulu for educational purposes.

Follow the road back to where it turns to cut across the valley. You pass the ruins of houses, the result of a devastating tidal wave. After you ford some shallow streams crossing the road, you approach some houses and a hotel on the right side. Nearby was once the location of a Peace Corps training area. Flooding in November 1979 destroyed the abandoned buildings that had served for training recruits who were going to serve in Asia.

There is no trail to Nanaue Falls, on the southwest side of the valley, but with a willingness to get wet, you can find your way to this delightful spot to picnic and to swim. Nanaue is really a number of falls, some with generous swimming holes at their bases. You have to climb around a bit to find the larger and deeper pools.

There are numerous cardinals (*Richmondena cardinalis*) in the valley, which flush from the trees as you make your way. The male, with its all-red body and its pointed crest, and the black-and-red female were introduced from the mainland.

Waipio to Waimanu, 7 miles one way, 6 hours (trail rating: difficult).

The most difficult part of the trek to Waimanu is the ascent up the northwest pali (cliff) of Waipio Valley. The trail is easy to find about 100 yards from the beach in a forest at the base of the northwest cliff. The switchbacks are steep but well-maintained. Obviously, this 1200-foot climb is best approached in the cool of the morning.

From the ridge, the trail crosses 14 gulches to Waimanu; so it's up and down you go along the pali overlooking the rugged coastline. There are places where some rock slides make the going a bit difficult and slow, so be cautious. The trail shelter is nine gulches from Waipio Valley, or about two-thirds of the way to Waimanu. It is a satisfactory place to lunch or camp, although you may have to share it with other hikers.

As you swing out of Pukoa (lit., "coral head") Gulch, you get your first view of Waimanu Valley. The similarity between Waipio and Waimanu will surprise you. Although Waimanu is only about half the size of Waipio, it contains a similar verdant valley and is bounded by precipitous cliffs. It's a sight to behold.

Waimanu Stream greets you on the floor of the valley after a steep descent. The best place to ford Waimanu Stream is about 25 feet above the spot where the stream joins the ocean. For drinking water, hike about ½ mile along the west side of the pali to an unnamed waterfall. Once again, either treat the water or boil it before drinking. There are numerous beach-front camping sites, so scout around and find one that suits you. As at Waipio, beware of ocean swimming because of the heavy surf with riptides.

There are no trails, since Waimanu, unlike Waipio, has long been abandoned, but you will find stone walls and foundations as well as taro terraces remaining from when it was occupied.

The jewel of Waimanu is Waiilikahi (lit., "water with single surface") Falls, about 1½ miles along the northwest pali of the valley. You must make your own trail to the falls. With luck, you'll arrive when the succulent mountain apples (*Eugenia malaccensis*) are ripe, usually in June. The fruit is a small red and pinkish apple with a thin, waxy skin. Its white flesh is crisp and juicy. Enjoy your lunch, the apples, and a swim in the large pool below the falls.

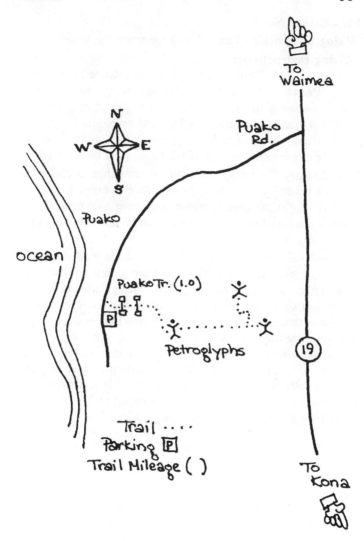

4 Puako Petroglyphs

Rating: Hardy family.
Features: Hawaiian petroglyphs.

Permission: None.

Hiking Distance & Time: 1 mile one-way, 1 hour.

Driving Instructions:

From Hilo (75 miles, 2 hours) west on Route 19, right at Puako sign. Look for Hawaiian Visitor Bureau marker near the end of the road, past house #153

From Kona (31 miles, 1 hour) north on Route 19, left at Puako sign. Look for Hawaiian Visitor Bureau marker near the end of the road, past house #153.

Introductory Notes: Petroglyphs are drawings or carvings on rock made by prehistoric or primitive people. Those at Puako (lit., "sugar cane blossom"), of unknown origin, are some of the finest examples on the islands, and probably the most numerous.

On the Trail: The trail to the petroglyphs is well-defined, but the painted markers on the lava seem to detract from the experience. It is a hot and dusty walk through a kiawe forest to the first set of petroglyphs, about 600 feet from the road. You pass through two gates. All the drawings and carvings are on pahoehoe lava, which has a smooth or ropy surface. The second and third groups are outstanding examples and are fun to puzzle out. While the meanings of some are obvious, others challenge the imagination. It is almost like browsing in a bookstore or in an antique store. You are irresistibly drawn to look and look and look.

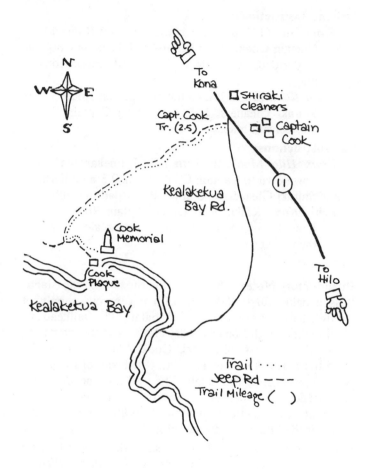

5 Captain Cook Monument

Rating: Strenuous. Elevation loss 500 feet.

Features: Site of Captain Cook's death, mango, papaya, avocodo, guava, ancient Hawaiian burial caves, swimming, snorkeling.

Permission: None.

Hiking Distance & Time: 2.5 miles one-way, 2 hours.

Driving Instructions:

> *From Hilo* (113 miles, 3 hours) west on Route 11 to
> Captain Cook, sharp left just past Captain Cook on
> Bay Road, 0.1 mile to jeep road (trail); consult
> map.

> *From Kona* (14 miles, ½ hour) south on Route 11 to
> Shiraki Cleaners, before reaching Captain Cook,
> etc. consult map.

Bus Instructions:

> *From Hilo* Mooheau Terminal, Kamehameha Ave.
> downtown to Captain Cook. Walk 0.3 mile north to
> Shiraki Cleaners and down Bay Road to trailhead.

> *From Kona* Kailua Post Office, Palani Rd. (opposite
> Kona Coast shopping center) to Captain Cook and
> then as above.

Introductory Notes: This is my favorite hike on the island.
It is a delightful ½-day trek with a generous supply of
nature's best fruits to suit anyone's palate. The trailhead is a
bit difficult to find. Look for a dry cleaners on the main road
just north of the town of Captain Cook. Almost opposite the
store the road to Kealakekua (lit., "pathway of the god")
Bay drops abruptly to the left. The trail itself begins about
500 feet down this road. It is a jeep road, at the start of which
is a giant jacaranda tree with violet-blue blossoms. Find the
trail, for the hike is worth the effort.

On the Trail: You should carry a small daypack to load up
on fruits along the first ½ mile. Mango (*Mangifera indica*) is
particularly abundant in the fields and along the roadside.
Look under the trees for those that have fallen and are not
too badly bruised, or find a stick to shake some loose from
the trees. If you find a good long stick, leave it near the trail
for the next hiker.

One of the favorite fruits of visitors and locals is the
papaya (*Carica papaya*). The ripe yellow fruit varies in size,
but can be found growing in clusters at the bases of
umbrellalike leaves. In ancient Hawaii, the leaves were used

as soap and as a meat tenderizer, and the seeds were used medicinally. You will find numerous papaya trees along the roadside.

As if this weren't enough, there are also some avocado (*Persea americana*) trees. Their fruit tends to be too watery for some people's tastes, but perhaps not for yours.

Do not pick fruit in the area near the small coffee farm on the right a few hundred yards from the start of the trail. There is no point in evoking the owner's anger.

The jeep road is infrequently used and is, therefore, overgrown with tall elephant grass, so that the tread is somewhat obscured, but it is still easy to follow. The trail is heavily overgrown for the first mile. As you approach the coast, the terrain becomes more arid, sustaining only low scrub. You have your first view of the coast, a part of Kealakekua Bay, and your destination—although the Cook Memorial is not visible. Bear left toward the beach at the first junction in the road. From here, go straight on to the beach. When you reach the beach, follow the coast to the left for a few hundred feet to the memorial. You needn't be concerned about the tourist boats' disturbing your visit, for the passengers do not disembark. The boats simply make a pass by the memorial and anchor in the bay for people who wish to snorkel for a short time. Locals claim that the fishing and the skin diving are outstanding here.

There are numerous caves—some containing human bones—beyond the monument and along the walls of the cliff. If you choose to explore, do not disturb any interesting finds. A number of local people are seeking to preserve what may be ancient Hawaiian burial grounds.

The docking area in front of the monument is a good place to picnic and to swim. If you explore the beach where the jeep road ends, you should find the original plaque commemorating the death of Captain Cook, usually under a foot or so of water. This the spot where Captain James Cook, who was the first white man to discover the Islands, was killed in 1779 while attempting to end a fight between his men and the Hawaiians.

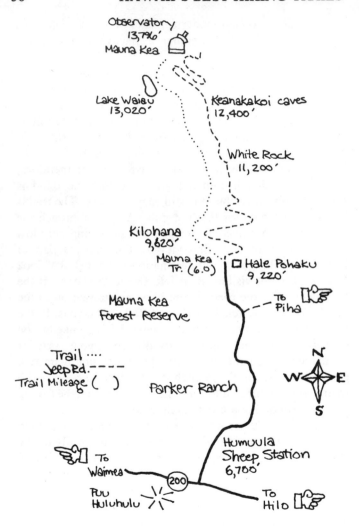

6 Mauna Kea Summit

Rating: Difficult. Elevation gain 4176 feet.
Features: Highest point on Hawaii.

Permission: Permits for state cabins and/or access road to Hale Pohaku: Dept. of Land & Natural Resources.

Hiking Distance & Time: 6 miles one-way, 5 hours.

Driving Instructions:

From Hilo (35 miles, 1 hour) west on Route 200, right at Humuula Junction to Hale Pohaku (9620 feet).

From Kona (62 miles, 2 hours) north on Route 190, right on Route 200, left at Humuula Junction to Hale Pohaku (9620).

Introductory Notes: The hike to Hawaii's highest point (13,796) is not as difficult as it might appear at first glance. There are both a hiking trail and a jeep road to the summit and to the observatory. Indeed, in an ordinary passenger car it is possible to drive to the 9620-foot level, and farther in a four-wheel-drive vehicle. You should make your ascent and descent in one day because no camping is permitted and there are no trail shelters or cabins. Begin your ascent early in the morning while it is still cool at lower elevations. Since snow is common at higher elevations, with temperatures dipping to 15° F in winter, dress warmly even in summer and wear sound hiking boots. Remember, if you are going to drive to the 9620-foot level you must contact the Division of State Parks for permission and for a key to the gate. However, the gate is usually open on work days.

On the Trail: From the trailhead at Hale Pohaku (lit., "stone house") the foot trail ascends northwestward and the jeep road northeastward. Since the cinder jeep road is firmer and more gradually sloped than the foot trail, you may choose to take it to the summit and return via the foot path. The trail is well-defined by steel posts and ahus (stone cairns).

You may see a number of birds common to this area. Be on the lookout for the large (three-foot-long) ring-necked pheasant (*Phasianus colchicus torquatus*) and the smaller chukar (*Alectoris graeca*), with its brownish-black markings and a black band extending through each eye and joining at the lower throat. Californians should recognize the common

California quail (*Lophortiyx californicus*), with its striking black plume and its bluish-gray breast and brown backing.

As you ascend, look south for startling views of the saddle (the area between Mauna Kea and Mauna Loa) and of Mauna Loa beyond. The altitude and the gradient will test your lungs and legs, and stops will be frequent. The first couple of miles are steep and difficult, until you reach "White Rock," a large outcropping of rock painted white, at 11,200 feet.

The trail from here to Lake Waiau (lit., "swirling water") (13,020 feet) is considerably easier. At the 12,000-foot level, be on the lookout for a trail that leads to the Keanakakoi (lit., "cave of the adzes") Caves, where ancient Hawaiians mined the stones for their adzes. It is a National Historic Landmark and the world's most extensive ancient adze quarry. It is a short ¼ mile from the jeep road.

At Lake Waiau you are about 700 feet from the summit. The lake, 400 feet across and 15 feet deep, is a rather remarkable phenomenon, for an impervious bottom in an otherwise porous lava area keeps the water from seeping away. This is the highest lake in the United States.

The summit of Mauna Kea (lit., "white mountain") is a cluster of cones from which Haleakala on the island of Maui is sometimes visible to the northwest. The observatory here is operated by the University of Hawaii in cooperation with the U.S. Air Force and NASA.

Kauai

The Island

Some people call it Kauai-a-mamo-ka-lani-po—"The fountainhead of many waters from on high and bubbling up from below." Others regard it as "The Grand Canyon of the Pacific" or "The Garden Island" and still others say it is "The land of the Menehune." But even if you just call it "Kauai"—meaning time of plenty, or fruitful season—it is still an land of beauty, grandeur and adventure, and a challenge to the outdoorsman. There is a lot of hiking pleasure packed into this almost circular little island of 555 square miles.

Kauai lays claim to a number of firsts and unique characteristics. It is the oldest island in the Hawaiian Islands, it is the northernmost inhabited island in the chain, and it was the first one visited by Captain Cook—though that is a rather dubious distinction. Still other things of local pride include Mt. Waialeale, the wettest spot on earth; the only place on earth where the iliau, a rare and unique plant, is to be found; and the home of the legendary Menehune, a race of pygmies who were short, industrious, strong, and highly skilled workers in stone.

As on the neighboring islands, tourism on Kauai with its 39,000 inhabitants has grown to the point that over 800,000 people annually visit it. Kauai lies 102 air miles northwest of Honolulu—about a 20-minute flight. Most visitors to Kauai are seeking its solitude and slower pace of life, and many find these in the verdant valleys of the remote Na Pali coast and in the lush canyon lands of Waimea. Conveniently, the State of Hawaii and the County of Kauai have established miles of trails and jeep roads into remote areas which will reveal some of the island's secrets.

Lihue is the center of tourist activity and the county seat. (Kauai is a county.) There is no public transportation on the

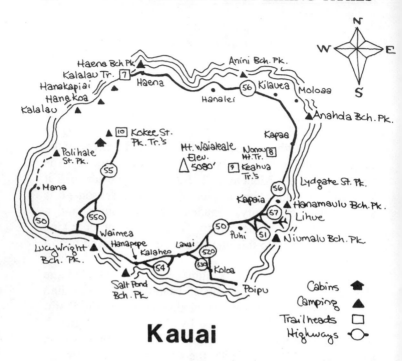

Kauai

island. At present, hitchhiking is allowed, although the county council raises the issue from time to time, and may prohibit it in the future. Check with the information booth at the airport regarding the law. If you hitchhike, be patient, for rides are hard to come by in the outlying areas.

Camping

Campgrounds on Kauai range from adequate to good, contain most of the amenities, and are either free or cheap. The accompanying map locates and cites the facilities available at state and county campgrounds. A third jurisdiction, the Division of Forestry, also provides a number of campgrounds, camping shelters, and camping areas, which are noted on individual maps throughout this chapter. A word about each kind of campground should be helpful.

First, the Hawaii State Parks at Kokee and Polihale offer excellent facilities and are free. Camping is limited to 5 days within a 30-day period for each campground, and is by permit only. The Division of State Parks also regulates camping along the Na Pali coast: Hanakapiai, Hanakoa, Kalalau—the three major valleys along the wilderness trail. Camping here is also limited to 5 days within a 30-day period. Camping at Hanakapiai and Hanakoa is limited to one night each, with the other 3 days allowed at Kalalau.

When writing for reservations, include the dates desired, the park, the number of persons and their names. The state cabins at Kokee State Park are operated by a concessionaire (See Hiking Area No. 10 for details).

Second, the County of Kauai has numerous campgrounds and beach parks around the island. County camping costs $3 per adult per day. Persons under 18 are free if accompanied by an adult. Permits are not issued to persons under 18. Camping permits are issued for four days, and can be renewed for four more. No person will be issued a permit for more than 12 days during any one year. When writing for reservations include your name, address, campground desired, dates, number of persons in your party, with names and ages, and the $3 fee per adult per day. Although reservations may be made by mail, all permits must be picked up in person at the County Portable Building #5 in Lihue or, when closed, at the Kauai Police Department nearby.

Last, the Hawaii State Division of Forestry maintains a number of trailside camping areas in the forest reserve, which are identified on the individual maps preceding the text of each hiking area on Kauai. Camping is limited to 3 nights within a 30-day period. Neither permits nor reservations are necessary. Registration is by sign-in at the trailhead upon entering and leaving a forest-reserve area. All the facilities are primitive and lacking in amenities, but to some people that is their best feature.

My advice is to stay at the state parks—Kokee or

Polihale—when possible, for they are conveniently situated, the best campgrounds on the island, and free. Of the county campgrounds, Salt Pond is very good Haena and Hanamaulu are satisfactory.

Campers are well advised to bring their own equipment because locally it is expensive. There are two equipment rental companies on the island. Bob's Bargain Rentals is located near the airport in Nawiliwili and Hanalei Camping and Backpacking is located in Hanalei. One alternative is to rent a fully equipped camper, which provides both your transportation and your camping equipment. For information write Beach Boy Campers. Mobile homes and campers are permitted only at Kokee and Polihale state parks, and at Haena, Hanamaulu and Niumalu county parks.

All addresses appear in the Appendix.

Hiking

With the exceptions of the Kalalau Trail and some of the trails in the Kokee/Waimea hiking area, hiking on Kauai does not require any special equipment or skill. Many places are readily accessible even to the tenderfoot and to the people not inclined to hike much. Few people dispute that the Kalalau Trail is an outstanding outdoor experience requiring good physical condition and backpacking equipment. However, the first two miles of the trail to Hanakapiai Valley and beach can be made by most people of any age who are willing to sweat a bit. Even so, wear good boots or tennis shoes and carry water.

If time allows, spend at least three days at Kokee State Park. The housekeeping cabins and the campground are comfortable, and the outstanding hiking experiences include hikes to suit everyone's interest and ability.

Water is available from streams in many areas, but it should be boiled or treated before drinking. Cattle, pigs and goats usually share the stream water with you. I suggest you begin each hike with one quart of water per person. Due to the heavy rainfall on Kauai, dry firewood is rare, so a small, light, reliable backpacking stove is a convenience and a comfort. A hot cup of tea, coffee or soup is invigorating while waiting out a passing storm, and a hot breakfast is desirable after a wet night. Lastly, most hikers find shorts or cutoffs adequate on most trails. However, along the Kalalau Trail most people shed all clothing for either physical or psychological reasons—I have not decided which.

7 Kalalau Trail

Rating: Difficult. Elevation gain 2000 feet.

Features: Wilderness area, views, fruits, waterfalls, swimming, historical sites.

Permission: Camping permits are required for Hanakapiai, Hanakoa and Kalalau valleys. Permits for camping must be obtained from the Division of State Parks.

Hiking Distance & Time: 10.8 miles one-way, 8 hours.

Driving Instructions:
38 miles, 1 hour from Lihue. North on Route 56 to road's end.

Introductory Notes: When people talk about hiking on Kauai they talk about visiting the uninhabited valleys of the Na Pali ("the cliffs") Coast, as evidenced by the comments registered by hikers on the sign-in at the trailhead—for example, "fantastic," "incredible," "Paradise," "the most beautiful place in the world." The Kalalau ("the straying") Trail to the end of the beach (10.8 miles) is the most exciting hike on the island. Until recently Kalalau Valley was part of the Makaweli ("fearful features") Ranch, which is owned by the Robinson family. The valley, the beach, and the Na Pali coastal lands now have state-park status and are under the jurisdiction and management of the Department of Land and Natural Resources, Division of State Parks.

Few who have hiked the Kalalau Trail will deny its grandeur and its captivating allure. Cliffs rise precipitously above the blue-green water and the rugged, rocky, north shore of Kauai. The valleys of the Na Pali Coast are

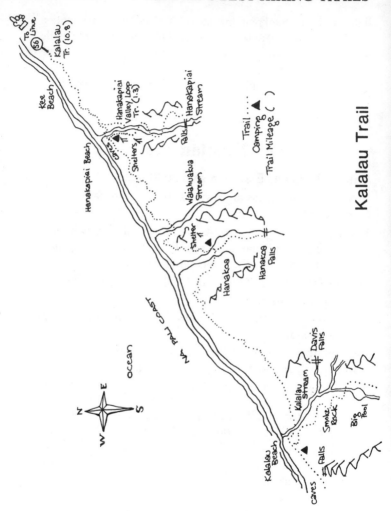

Kalalau Trail

accessible only by foot or by boat, and only during the summer when the tides expose a generous sandy beach which is ripped away each year by winter storms. In the summer of 1981, the trail was in good condition except for the area between the 3 and 6 mile markers. Numerous slides and fallen trees made the trail there quite hazardous, but passable with caution.

Special Instructions. Hiking the whole trail to Kalalau requires backpacking equipment for a comfortable, safe trip. Sound hiking boots are essential, since a good deal of your hiking is on soft cinders and ash along the precipitous coast and on rocky trail in the valleys. A strong, waterproof tent is needed to stand up under the wind at Kalalau and the rain at Hanakoa. Although fresh water is available all along the trail, you should boil or treat the water: other people, goats and pigs are using the same stream. A light sleeping bag is adequate, particularly during the summer months, when the nighttime temperature is very comfortable. Little if any clothing is necessary during the day, and it is common to find persons of both sexes hiking without any. A backpacking stove is recommended since dry firewood is difficult to find and tree cutting is not permitted. The trailhead for the Kalalau Trail is at the end of the road, where it is possible to park your car. A word of caution, however, may save some grief: in recent years a number of break-ins have been reported, so don't leave anything in the car, and leave it unlocked.

A state park ranger is in residence in Kalalau. He does check for permits, in addition to his other duties.

Kee Beach to Hanakapiai Beach, 2 miles.

The trek to Hanakapiai (lit., "bay sprinkling food") Beach is an honest hike; it is one steep mile up and one steep mile down from Kee (lit., "avoidance") Beach. This is a much frequented trail because tourist publications promise a verdant valley resplendent with native and introduced flora. No one is disappointed. Particularly abundant is the hala (*Pandanus tectorius*), an indigenous tree that grows in coastal areas. It is sometimes called "tourist pineapple," since the fruit resembles a pineapple and is jokingly identified as such by locals for tourists. Humor aside, the hala has been a valuable resource, the hollow trunk of the female tree being used as a pipe for drainage between taro patches. The leaves have commercial value, being used for weaving many items such as basket, mats and hats—hats being particularly popular with tourists.

The first half mile up the cliff provides views at a couple of points back to Kee Beach and Haena ("wilderness") reefs. This part of the trail is usually shady because of the large trees and cool because of the trade winds and periodic rain showers. One source of shade is the large kukui (*Aleurites moluccana*) tree, from the nuts of which a beautiful and popular lei is made. To make a lei, each nut must be sanded, filed and polished to a brilliant luster, which is imparted by its own oil. Until the advent of electricity, kukui-nut oil was burned for light. Nicknamed the "candle-nut tree" its trunk was shaped into canoes by early Hawaiians.

A wide, well-maintained trail leads up and down from the ½ to the 1¼ mile marker. With any luck you may find some sweet guava (*Psidium guajava*), a small yellow, lemon-sized fruit that is perhaps better in juice or jam form. Before eating one, break it open and check for worms. They are tiny and are a little hard to see but are common in wild guava.

Near the 1-mile marker, look for a small springlet that flows year 'round and provides a thirst-quenching drink. At the 1½-mile marker, you'll have your first view of Hanakapiai Beach below, with its generous beach (during the summer months) and its crashing surf. Look for wild orchids, with their delicate purplish flowers, thriving along the banks of the trail.

On your descent to the beach, about three-quarters of the way down, the Hanakapiai Loop Trail goes left. It is 2 miles to the base of Hanakapiai Falls. You may continue on to the beach and take the west side of the loop into the valley. I suggest that you hike to the falls in the afternoon after a swim in the ocean or in the pools in Hanakapiai Stream. It is more likely to be warm and sunny in the valley and free of rain in the afternoon.

If you want to stay overnight at Hanakapiai Beach, you have a choice of campsites. There is a camping area on the beach along either side of the stream, and there are two Division of Forestry trail-crew shelters on the west side of the stream about ¼ and ¾ mile from the beach. Additionally, a number of large mango trees provide an idyllic and private campsite also on the west side off the loop trail. At low tide during the summer, you may prefer the unique experience of one of the cave campsites that are located on both the west and east ends of the beach. From Hanakapiai to Kalalau, you can expect considerable nudity. Indeed, you're pretty straight or different—depending on your point of view—if you're wearing clothes. Certainly the climate and the Eden-like setting seem to free one of any inhibitions he may have. You'll discover that there are a lot of healthy people on Kauai!

Hanakapiai Valley Loop Trail, 1.3 miles, 1 hour

The Hanakapiai Valley loop is an easy hike along the stream and through a rain forest resplendent with native flora. The beginning of the trail on the west side of the valley contains some of the largest mango (*Mangifera indica*) trees anywhere. One grove surrounding the remains of a coffee mill contains a tree that is 23 feet in circumference. Obviously, it makes a shady, sheltered campsite. The mango tree is not native to Hawaii, but its many varieties have done well there, and are popular with locals and tourists. However, the trees in this valley do not bear as well as those in drier areas because of a fungus that kills the blossoms in wet areas. Many people regard the mango fruit as second to none in taste and appearance.

The stone-wall enclosures are the remains of ancient taro terraces where the taro plant was grown to provide Hawaiians with their staple, poi. Hundreds of varieties of taro have been recorded from which poi, a thick paste, is produced. Poi is made from the tubers (roots), which are baked or boiled and then pounded by hand or machine. It may be eaten fresh or allowed to ferment for a few days, which adds a pleasant sour taste. Poi is traditionally eaten with the fingers along with pork or fish.

"Okolehau" ("Okole" is translated "anus" or "but-tocks;" and "hau" can mean "cool") is a Division of Forestry trail-crew shelter near the coffee mill, which you may use when it is not occupied by a trail crew.

At the ½-mile marker the loop trail turns left to cross the stream and return to the beach. It is a little wetter on the east side and the trail is more difficult to follow since it is overgrown with a variety of flora including both common and strawberry guava fruit; ti, whose leaves provide hula dancers with their skirts; coffee, with tiny green or red berries; and the beautiful, fragrant, delicate ginger. Continue on to the main trail and return to the beach for a swim in the ocean or in the freshwater pools in the stream.

Hanakapiai Falls Trail from Hanakapiai Valley Loop Trail, 1.3 miles.

The hike to the falls is a must not only because the falls are spectacular, but also because much serenity and enchantment are to be found in the valley. The first ¼ mile is an easy trail that snakes along the stream. If the stream is high or if it is raining hard, you should not attempt to hike to the falls, for the trail narrows considerably in the upper portions and flash flooding is a serious consideration. Just before the ¾-mile marker you cross the stream. If the crossing is difficult due to high water, that is a good clue that you should not continue until the water has receded. Beyond this crossing, the trail continues up the opposite bank. You will make three stream crossings. The trail is always easy to find because the valley is so narrow. In this lower area, there are traces of abandoned taro terraces. The last ½ mile is the most difficult part, but perhaps the most enchanting, with inviting pools and slides and verdant growth. The trail is cut into the walls of the canyon in a number of places, and caution is well-advised. Although the pool at the base of the falls is inviting, caution is again advised for there is danger from falling rocks from the cliffs and the ledge above the falls. Hanakapiai Falls cascades and falls about 300 feet in the back of a natural amphitheater. You don't need to be told to swim and enjoy the pools and the surrounding area. You will find safe pools away from falling rocks.

Hanakapiai to Hanakoa, 4 miles, 2½ hours.

Serious hiking on the trail to Kalalau begins at this point as the trail climbs out of Hanakapiai Valley on a series of switchbacks for one mile. Hiking here in the morning means that the sun will be at your back and, with the trade wind, it should be relatively cool. The trail does not drop to sea level again until Kalalau Beach, some nine miles along the cliffs.

There are two small valleys before Hanakoa. The first is Hoolulu (lit., "to lie in sheltered waters"), which is first viewed from a cut in the mountain at the 3¼-mile marker. From here you descend to cross the valley and climb the opposite side. Hoolulu is thickly foliated with native and introduced plants that are typical of most valleys on the island. Ti, guava, morning glory, mountain orchids, and different kinds of ferns can be identified along with the larger kukui, koa and hala trees. Be careful at points where the trail narrows along a precipitous slope. In 1981 there were numerous slides across the trail and parts of the trail were heavily overgrown between the 3¼ and 5¾ mile markers. There is also a danger of falling rocks.

Waiahuakua Valley, at the 4¼-mile marker, is broader than Hoolulu. In August, with any luck, you are likely to find delicious ohia ai (*Eugenia malaccensis*), or mountain apples, growing along the trail. Abundant in Waiahuakua, these trees have smooth, dark green leaves and some attain a height of 50 feet. The fruit is a small red or pinkish apple with a thin, waxen skin, while the meat is flesh-white, crisp and juicy, with a large brown seed in the center—a very tasty repast for those lucky enough to find some. Additionally, the valley abounds in coffee, ti, guava, kukui and mango.

At the 5¾-mile marker, you get your first view of Hanakoa (lit., "bay of koa trees, or of warriors") Valley which is a broad-terraced valley that was once cultivated by Hawaiians. Many of the terraced areas provide relatively sheltered camping sites. In addition, "Mango Shelter" has a roof-and-table camp and "Hanakoa Shack" a short distance

away, is a Division of Forestry trail-crew shelter that is open
to hikers when not in use by crews. Both are located along
the trail a short distance into the valley. Camping in
Hanakoa is quite an experience since it receives frequent
rains, and as soon as you dry out, it rains again. However,
the afternoon can be warm and sunny, just perfect for a swim
in one of the many pools in the stream and a sunbath on the
large, warm rocks along the bank. These are a favorite of
nude sun worshippers. If you plan to camp in Hanakoa, be
prepared for a lot of rain, wetness and humidity. To
compensate, you will have solitude and your own private
swimming pool.

To Hanakoa Falls, .4 mile one way, ¼ hour.

Extreme caution should be exercised when hiking to
Hanakoa Falls. A 40-foot section of the cliff recently slid
200 feet down to the rocky streambed. The trail begins
between the stream crossing and the 6½-mile marker and
passes a wilderness campsite area.

Hanakoa to Kalalau Beach, 4.8 miles, 3 hours.

Your physical condition and your hiking skill will be
tested on this, the most difficult part of the Kalalau Trail.
Not only is most of the hiking on switchbacks that alternate
up and down along a very precipitous cliff, but also the danger
is increased by a number of slides along the trail. Another
hazard is the hot afternoon sun—unless you begin hiking
early. However, the rewards are great. Indeed, the views of
the northwest coastline are absolutely breathtaking and
staggeringly beautiful. It is difficult to think of another view
in the world that compares.

At the 6½-mile marker, you enter land that until 1975
was part of the Makaweli (lit., "fearful features") cattle
ranch. The area becomes increasingly dry as you continue
west, and only the smaller, more arid types of vegetation survive, like sisal and lantana. Lantana (*Lantana camara*) is a
popular flower that blossoms almost continuously. Its flowers
vary in color from yellow to orange to pink to red; infrequently, they are white with a yellow center. If you hike in the

early morning or late afternoon you're likely to frighten feral goats foraging near the trail and near some of the small streams along the trail.

Although there are only a few trail-mileage markers over the rest of the route, there is no chance of getting lost. The trail is over open land and is visible ahead. There are at least five reliable sources of water between Hanakoa and Kalalau. The admonition to treat or to boil the water applies.

Pohakuao (lit., "day stone") is the last small valley before Kalalau. As you ascend the west side of Pohakuao along a pali with sparse foliage and reddish earth, you get your first view of Kalalau, a welcome sight after a difficult three miles from Hanakoa. There is no mistaking Kalalau, for it is a large, broad valley some two miles wide and three miles long. From the ridge, a precipitous snakelike trail drops abruptly to Kalalau Stream, where a rushing creek and cool pools await the weary hiker.

Camping is allowed only on the beach, in the trees fronting the beach and in the caves at the far end of the beach. Try to find a spot that will shelter you from the strong winds and the hot daytime sun. Some campers find shelter in the low scrub along the beach during the day and then sleep on the beach during the cool and usually wind-free nights. Lantana and common guava are particularly abundant along the trail in the beach area. You should easily find some ripe guava to add to your meals. Don't drink the stream water until you boil or treat it. The falls at the end of the beach by the caves is your best bet for safe water although it is a good idea to boil or to treat that water also. The water from the falls also serves the feral goats that you will undoubtedly see in the morning or at dusk when they visit to refresh themselves. The falls also make for a pleasant shower, with a small bathing pool at the base.

Kalalau Beach to Big Pool, 2 miles one way, 1½ hour.

The best trail into the valley begins on the west side of Kalalau Stream at the marked trailhead. Before heading into the valley, hike to the top of the knoll above the beach, also on the west side of the stream. The remains of a heiau—a pre-Christian place of worship—lie between the knoll and the beach and are clearly identifiable from this vantage point. Little is known about this nameless heiau. Remember that such places are still revered by many people, and a rock wrapped in a ti leaf and left on a heiau site is believed to protect the traveler.

From the trailhead, the trail parallels the stream for a short distance and then ascends an eroded rise. From here the trail alternately passes open and forested areas. In the wooded areas look for oranges, mango, common guava and rose apple. Each is common in the valley and can supplement a backpackers diet. At the one-mile point, Smoke Rock is a convenient place to pause in an open area from which the entire valley can be viewed. This is the place where the valley marijuana growers and residents used to meet to smoke and to talk stories. The rest of the trail to Big Pool is under the shade of giant mango and rose apple trees. Before reaching Big Pool, a side stream crossing must be made. Our trail then meets a trail which to the left leads to Kalalau Stream and to the beach, and to the right leads to Big Pool. Heading into the valley, the next stream crossing is Kalalau Stream. Big Pool, a short distance from this crossing, is easily identified. Two room-sized pools are separated by a natural water slide which is a joy to slip down into the cool water below. It is a "relatively" smooth slide!

Kalalau Beach to Davis Falls, 1 mile from Big Pool.

In 1984, a group of island Boy Scouts and Explorer Scouts cut a trail from the stream near big pool to Davis Falls. The trailhead is at a point just above the last major stream crossing before big pool, and it is posted 'Davis Falls 0.9 miles.' The trail passes through heavy brush until it reaches a pool at the base of the upper falls. The falls are named for Richard Davis, an outdoorsman who has explored the valley for many years. The falls are a marvelous place to swim or shower and to pause to enjoy the sights and smells of Kalalau, Kauai's most precious treasure.

Kalalau abounds in a variety of life. Beach naupaka (*Scaevola frutescens*), with small, fragrant, white flowers, can be found near the beach, mixed with the low sisal and lantana. Hala, ti, ferns, bamboo, bananas, mango, kukui, monkeypod and many other species of flora can be identified. Rock terraces where Hawaiians planted taro as late as the 1920's are also common.

Some very daring people attempt to wade and swim around the point where the beach ends on the west in an effort to visit Honopu (lit., "conch bay") Valley, the so-called "Valley of the Lost Tribe"—a reference to the legendary little people named Mu who once lived there. Interestingly, the remains of an ancient settlement have been found in the valley. We don't know who left them, but there's no evidence it was the Mu people. However, the swim around the point takes about 15 minutes and is very risky due to the strong current and undertow in the ocean. If you must see Honopu Valley, better charter a boat or a helicopter in Lihue.

Locals and visitors enjoy speculating about the exploits and the hideouts of Kalalau's most famous citizen, Koolau. Commonly called "Koolau the Leper," this native Hawaiian was born in Kekaha in 1862. Three years after showing signs of leprosy, at the age of 27, Koolau and the other lepers of Kauai were ordered to the leper colony on Molokai, and were promised that their wives and children could accompany them. When the ship sailed without his wife and child, Koolau, realizing he had been tricked, dove overboard and swam ashore. Together with his wife and child he made the perilous descent into Kalalau Valley to join other lepers who sought to escape deportation. A year later, local authorities decided to round up the lepers, all of whom agreed to go to Molokai except Koolau. A sheriff's posse exchanged fire with Koolau, who shot and killed a deputy. Martial law was declared, and a detachment of the national guard was sent from Honolulu with orders to get their man dead or alive. A small cannon was mounted near the site where Koolau was thought to be hiding. In the ensuing "battle" Koolau shot two guardsmen and one accidentally shot and killed himself while fleeing the leper. The remaining guardsmen fled from the valley to the beach. In the morning they blasted Koolau's hideout with their cannon. Believing him dead, the guardsmen left the valley. But Koolau had moved his family the night before the cannonading, and they lived in the valley for about five more years, always fearful that the guard was still looking for him. They hid during the day and hunted for food at night. Tragically, their son developed signs of leprosy and soon died; a year later, the dread disease claimed Koolau. Piilani, his wife, buried her husband in the valley that had become their home along with his gun which had enabled them to be together to the end.

To some, Koolau is a folk hero who received unfair treatment by the government. Indeed, locals claim that Koolau frequently left his valley hideout to visit friends and relatives on Kauai. Whatever the facts, it makes for an interesting story and campfire conversation.

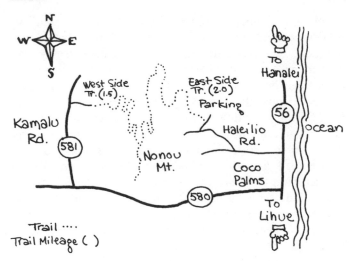

8 Nonou Mountain (Sleeping Giant)

Rating: Hardy family.

Features: Views of Kauai, fruits.

Permission: None.

Hiking Distance & Time: Consult individual hikes.

Hiking Instructions:

East Side 7 miles, ¼ hour from Lihue. North from Lihue on Route 56 past Coco Palms Hotel, left on Haleilio Road for 1.2 miles, park off road by sign *Nonou Trail.*

West Side 10 miles, ½ hour from Lihue. North from Lihue on Route 56, left on Route 580, right on Route 581 (Kamalu Road) for 1.2 miles to trailhead sign *Nonou Trail* opposite 1055 Kamalu Road.

Introductory Notes: There are two routes to the summit of Nonou (lit., "throwing") mountain, both of which are good, well-maintained trails that will take you to the giant's chin and to his forehead. Nonou is truly one of the best hikes on Kauai. Be certain to carry one quart of water since it is a hot hike in spite of frequent trade winds.

Nonou Mountain is known as the "sleeping giant" to tourists, and as "Puni" in Hawaiian folklore. It is told that the giant Puni lived among the legendary small folk, the Menehune, but was so clumsy that he continually knocked down their homes and their stone walls. Nevertheless, he was so friendly that the Menehune could not help but like him. One day the little people were faced with an invasion, and they went to the giant in the hope that the would destroy their enemies. However, they found him asleep on a ridge near Kapaa (lit., "the solid or the closing"). In an effort to awaken him, they threw large rocks on his stomach, which rebounded toward the ocean, destroying some of the invading canoes and causing the others to flee. In the morning they tried to awaken Puni again, only to discover that some of the rocks they had thrown at him had landed in his mouth. Tragically, he had swallowed them and died in his sleep.

East-side trail, 2 miles one-way, 1½ hours, elevation gain 1250 feet.

You can drive up the short access road to the water-filtration plant and park. The marked trailhead is across a drainage ditch. The trail is basically a series of well-defined switchbacks on the northeast side of the mountain. DO NOT hike on the southeast side, for it is extremely dangerous and precipitous. Pause frequently and enjoy the vistas overlooking the east side of Kauai. Below you lie the Wailua Houselots, while the Wailua River and the world famous Coco Palms resort are to your front right. There are ¼ mile trail markers along the entire route.

The large trees that flourish in the area not only offer a relatively shady trail, but also provide some shelter from showers, which are common. You will find guava, ti, tree ferns, a variety of eucalyptus, and others that deserve special note.

The hau tree (*Hibiscus tiliaceus*) is of particular interest, not because of its pretty bright-yellow blossom but because of its long, sinuous branches, which interlock to form an impenetrable barrier. Locals jokingly note that the tree is appropriately named (hau, pronounced how) because where they are plentiful, no one knows "hau" to pass through!

On a spacious overlook at about the one-mile-point, you can rest in the shade of the ironwood tree (*Casuarina equisetifolia*), which resembles a pine because of its long, slender, drooping, dull-green needles. It is an introduced tree that has a long life and is very useful as a windbreak or a shade tree.

Just beyond the 1½-mile marker, the west-side trail merges with ours for the ascent to the summit. Alii (lit., "chief") Shelter and Table at the 1¾-mile marker is a pleasant place to picnic and to enjoy the panorama of the island and the solitude. There are a number of benches near the shelter that provide comfortable places to meditate. You should see a white-tailed tropic bird (*Phaethon lepturus*) as it soars along the mountainside with its conspicuous 16-inch tail streamers. From the shelter, walk south through the monkeypod trees to survey the trail to the giant's chin, nose and forehead that leads a short ½ mile to the summit. Look over the trail and judge your ability to walk across a narrow ridge above a nearly vertical 500-foot cliff, to scramble up about 50 feet on your hands and knees to the "chin," and to walk about 150 yards along a narrow ridge to the "forehead." In spite of the hazard, the views of the island are compensation.

West-side trail, 1.5 miles, 1 hour, elevation gain 1000 feet.

The west-side trail is a bit shorter and not as steep, and offers more shade than the east-side trail. This trail passes by Queen's Acres and across a cattle range before entering the forest reserve. You will hike through a variety of introduced trees much like those found on the east side.

Look for the wild, or Philippine, orchid (*Spathoglottis plicata*). The wild variety is usually lavender, with what appear to be five starlike petals, but are actually two petals and three sepals.

The trails join at the 1½-mile marker for the short trek to Alii Shelter and on to the summit.

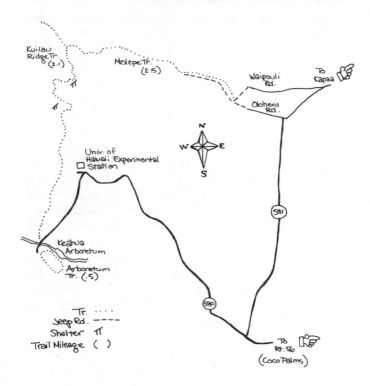

9 Keahua Trails

Rating: See individual hikes.

Features: Swimming hole, native and introduced plants, fruits.

Permission: None.

Hiking Distance & Time: See individual hikes.

Driving Instructions:

to Keahua Arboretum and Kuilau trails 12 miles, ½ hour from Lihue.

North on Route 56, left on Route 580 to University of Hawaii Agriculture Experiment Station, left on paved road 1.8 miles to Keahua Stream. Kuilau

Ridge Trailhead is on the right at a small turnout just before the stream and Keahua Arboretum Trailhead on the left just past the stream opposite a large parking area.

to Moalepe Trail 12 miles, ½ hour from Lihue.

North from Lihue on Route 56, left on Route 580, right on Route 581, for 1.6 miles, left on Olohena Road for 1.6 miles to pavement end and intersection with Waipouli Road. Park on shoulder of road.

Introductory Notes: The three hiking trails in the Keahua area offers some pleasureable experiences. They offer some marvelous views of the eastside coastline and of the Makaleha Mountains. Since the Moalepe Trail intersects the Kuilau Ridge Trail, you have an opportunity to follow the latter trail to Keahua Arboretum. If you can manage the shuttle transportation, a good 4.5-mile hike can be made by taking the Kuilau Ridge Trail to the Moalepe Trail and following it to the Olohena/Waipouli Road junction off Route 581.

Keahua Arboretum, .5 miles, ½ hour, (hike rating: family).

Keahua (lit., "the mound") Arboretum is a project of the Hawaii State Department of Land and Natural Resources, Division oï Forestry. Here is a good chance to view a variety of native and introduced plants and to swim in a cool, freshwater pool. The arboretum receives an annual average rainfall of 95 inches. The State Forest Reserve area extends west to the top of Mt. Waialeale ("overflowing water"), the highest spot on Kauai and the wettest place on earth, with an average annual rainfall of 468 inches. It once received a record 628 inches!

The trail follows a series of numbered posts that correspond with the numbers and narrative in a leaflet offered by the Division of Forestry, *A Trailside Guide to the Keahua Forestry Arboretum.*

Moalepe Trail, 2.5 miles, 1½ hours (hike rating: hardy family). Elevation gain 500 feet.

On the Trail: Do not attempt to drive beyond the Olohena-Waipouli Road intersection because the road is deeply rutted and, when wet, very slippery. The first part of the trail is on a right-of-way dirt road over pasture land. The usually cloud-enshrouded Makaleha (lit., "eyes looking about as in wonder and admiration") Mountains rise majestically to the north-west. In fact, the State of Hawaii, Division of Forestry, which is in charge of the area, has plans to extend the trail to the top of the Makalehas. Be sure to pause to enjoy the panorama of the coastline, from Moloaa on the north to Lihue on the south. There are some guavas along the fence and even more in the pasture, which is private land. The trail is a popular equestrian route with riders who rent horses from the ranches in the area: evidence of this fact can be found on the trail!

The first mile is a gentle ascent in open country. Then the trail enters the forest reserve. Hereafter, the trail is bordered with a variety of plants and trees, including the wild, or Philippine, orchid, different types of ferns, eucalyptus trees and the popular ohia lehua, with its pretty red blossoms. In the forest reserve the road-trail narrows and begins to twist and turn along the ridge, with many small and heavily foliated gulches to the left and Moalepe (lit., "chick with comb") Valley to the right. You can expect rain and therefore a muddy trail to the end of the hike. The trail reaches a junction with the Kuilau Ridge trail on a flat, open area at the 2.1-mile point. The ridge trail to the south (left) descends to two trail shelters and eventually ends at Keahua Arboretum, 2.1 miles from the junction. There is a sheltered picnic site 0.2 mile south of the junction along the Kuilau Ridge Trail. From the junction the Moalepe Trail is a footpath that snakes northwestward for 0.4 mile along Kuilau Ridge to a lookout point from which an enchanting panorama awaits the hiker.

Kuilau Ridge Trail, 2.1 miles, 1½ hours (trail rating: hardy family).

One of the most scenic hiking trails on the island, the Kuilau ("to string together leaves or grass") Ridge Trail climbs the ridge from Keahua Arboretum to two vista-point picnic sites. From the trailhead to trail's end, an abundance of native and introduced plants greets the hiker. The ascent of the ridge is on a well-maintained foot and horse trail lined with hala, ti plants, from which hula skirts are fashioned, and the very pretty lavender wild, or Philippine, orchid. But the best prize is a couple of mountain apple trees on the left side of the trail a short distance up from the trailhead. Perhaps you'll find some apples, which are red or pink when ripe.

At the 1¼-mile point the trail reachs a large flat area and a trail shelter and a picnic site. It is a delightful spot for a pause to enjoy views of the many gulches and the Makaleha Mountains beyond. However, if you plan to picnic, continue on for 0.8 mile to the second trail shelter and picnic area. The trail to the second shelter passes through one of the most beautiful places on the whole island. The Kuilau Ridge Trail twists and turns on a razorback ridge past a number of small waterfalls. It is a treasure to savor. Before reaching the shelter, the trail crosses a footbridge at the bottom of a gulch and then ascends the ridge to a large flat area and the picnic spot. From here, the trail continues 0.2 mile to its junction with the Moalepe Trail.

10   Kokee State Park/Waimea Canyon

Rating: See individual hikes.

Features: Views of Waimea Canyon and Na Pali Coast, swimming, camping, iliau plant, rain forest, wilderness hiking, wild plums, waterfalls.

Permission: Get camping permit at Division of State Parks.

Hiking Distance & Time: See individual hikes.

Driving Instructions:

38 miles, 1½ hours from Lihue to Kokee State Park Headquarters. South on Route 50, right on Route 550 (Waimea Canyon Drive) past Waimea. In Kokee Park, Route 550 becomes State Route 55, although it is not posted as such.

Introductory Notes: Kokee (lit., "to bend or to wind") State Park and Waimea (lit., "reddish water") Canyon are the most popular hiking and camping areas on the island, for obvious reasons. Waimea Canyon has been called the "Grand Canyon of the Pacific." Kokee has numerous hiking trails and untold hunting trails that snake along the pali to otherwise remote and inaccessible places. Everyone is quite taken by the beauty and grandeur of Waimea Canyon. It is about one mile wide, 3600 feet deep, and 10 miles long. While it does not match the magnificence of the Grand Canyon, it has its own unique magic, with its verdant valleys, its lush tropical forest and its rare birds and flora.

Technically, this northwest corner of the island is under two state agencies, the Division of State Parks and the Division of Forestry, both of which are under the Hawaii State Department of Land and Natural Resources; and Kokee Lodge is operated by a private concessionaire. While the accommodations are not luxurious, they are very comfortable and in keeping with the surroundings.

The state cabins at Kokee, very popular with locals and tourists, do not require reservations, but they are advisable. Kokee Lodge is not really a lodge but rather 12 rustic cabins completely furnished with refrigerator, water heater, stove, cooking utensils, shower, linens, blankets, beds and fire-place. All you need is food, which is not available at Kokee. The nearest store is 20 miles away, in Kekaha. There is, however, a restaurant and cocktail lounge a short walk from the cabins, open from 8:30 a.m. to 5:30 p.m. and on Fridays and Saturdays for dinner 6-9 p.m. Each cabin will accommodate 6 persons at a very modest cost of $25 per day. Write to the lodge for complete information and reservations. Even one year in advance is not too soon to reserve a cabin.

At the north end of a shady, picturesque meadow, tent and trailer camping are available in the shade of tall eucalyptus trees. Camping, limited to one week, is free, including water, tables, barbecues, restrooms, and cold-water showers. There are a number of wilderness camping areas and shelters available (see the map and the trail descriptions below) under the jurisdiction of the Division of Forestry.

In recent years a controversy has existed over the future of the Kokee-Waimea area. Conservationists have sought Federal legislation to establish a national park so that the wilderness can be preserved in relatively pristine condition. Opponents of this proposal seek to retain the present status, because a national park would prohibit hunting, picking plums, and taking plants.

Whatever the future, whether your interest is hiking, hunting or sightseeing, no trip to Kauai is complete without a visit to Kokee and Waimea Canyon. Kokee is also the home of the rare mokihana berry (see the Pihea Trail below), the even rarer and beautiful iliau tree (see the Iliau Nature Loop Trail below) and the delicious Methley plum, which is ready for picking throughout the park in the late May and early June. The picking season is short because local people flock to the park and carry off buckets full of this delectable fruit. Your interests, physical condition, and length of stay at Kokee will help determine which hike you take. On the whole, trails in the general vicinity of park headquarters are relatively short and easy, while trails into Waimea Canyon, to the valley overlooks or into the Alakai Swamp are full-day

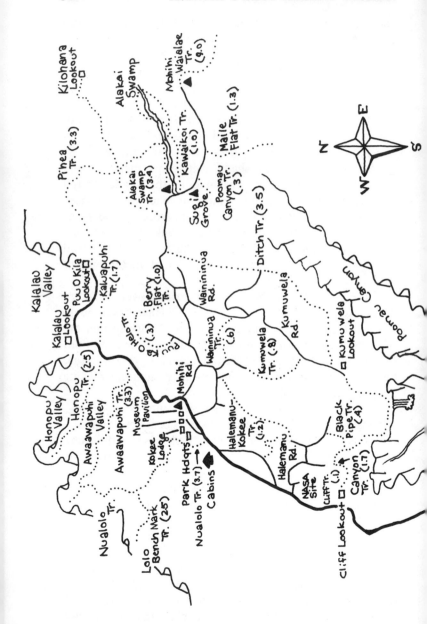

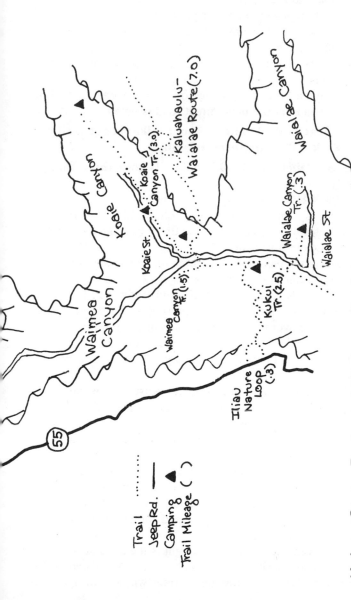

Kokee State Park and Waimea Canyon

Waialae Canyon

Waialae Canyon Tr. (.3)

Kaluahaulu–Waialae Route (7.0)

Waialae St.

Koaie Canyon

Koaie Canyon Tr. (3.0)

Koaie St.

Waimea Canyon

Waimea Canyon Tr. (1.5)

Kukui Tr. (2.5)

Iliau Nature Loop (.3)

55

Trail ....
Jeep Rd. ——
Camping ▲
Trail Mileage ( )

or overnight trips. Access to most of the trails is from jeep
roads that radiate off the main highway—Route 55. You cannot travel these jeep roads in a passenger car even when they
are dry. During the rainy season or after a heavy rain, only
four-wheel drive vehicles can do it. The ranger at park headquarters is the best source of information about road
conditions.

For each hike, the mileage from Park Headquarters to
the trailhead via the most direct road is noted.

Berry Flat Trail, 1 mile, ½ hour (hike rating: family).
   Park HQ to trailhead 1.2 miles.

Puu Ka Ohelo Trail, 0.3 mile, ¼ hour (hike rating:
family).
   Park HQ to trailhead 0.9 mile.

An easy, pleasant loop trail off Mohihi (a variety of
sweet potato) Road combines the Berry Flat and the Puu Ka
Ohelo (Ohelo hill) trails.

Both trails pass through scenic forest containing mostly
introduced trees that should be easy to identify. Particularly
noteworthy is a stand of California redwoods (*Sequoia
sempervirens*) that will excite the senses. These wondrous
giants tower over the other trees, adding a certain majesty to
the grove, and their droppings provide a luxuriant carpet on
which to walk. They are found as you begin the Berry Flat
Trail.

In addition, there are stands of Australian eucalyptus,
Japanese Sugi pines and the native koa (*Acacia koa*), which
grows to a height of more than 50 feet. The koa has a light
gray bark that is smooth on young trees and considerably
furrowed on mature trees. The leaves are smooth, stiff, and
crescent-shaped. Often called Hawaiian mahogany, the
wood is red with a wavy grain that makes it popular for use in
furniture, woodwork and ukuleles. In older times it had
nobler purposes, having been used for war canoes, surf-
boards and calabashes.

However, the prize to be sought is the popular Methley
plum, which flourishes in the Kokee area. At the end of the
Berry Flat Trail are a number of trees whose fruit ripens at

the end of May or the first part of June.

Although no markers are provided, both trails are clear, broad, and easy to follow. You will cross a couple of small streams as you turn onto the Puu Ka Ohelo Trail, where you will find a common vine which is a favorite of wild pigs. The banana passion fruit (*Passiflora mollissima*) is a wild vine that produces a pretty, light-pink blossom and a small, yellow, banana-shaped fruit. The Park Service regards the vine as a pest because it smothers native trees.

There is also a variety of birds along both trails. (All bookstores on the island have small, pocket-sized, inexpensive bird books featuring the most frequently seen birds). The cardinal (*Richmondena cardinalis*) is a commonly seen bird on the island which was introduced from the mainland. The male, with his all-red body and pointed crest, has been seen along both trails as well as throughout the park.

Canyon Trail, 1.7 miles, 2 hours (hike rating: strenuous). Elevation loss 800 feet.
Park HQ to trailhead 2.1 miles.

Although the Canyon Trail is steep in parts and requires some stamina, it offers some of the best views of Waimea Canyon. The trail begins off the Cliff Trail, about 50 feet from the end of Halemanu Road. Initially, the trail descends into a gulch, then emerges ¼ mile later on the east rim of Waimea Canyon. It is somewhat precipitous in places, so be careful. The trail snakes along the cliff a short distance and then goes southeast into a gulch and snakes along the cliff to Kokee Stream and Waipoo (lit., "head water") Falls, where you can picnic in the shade and swim or splash in the stream. Go up the stream a short distance for the best swimming hole.

A common plant on the high, dry ridges is the lantana (*Lantana camara*), which blooms almost continuously. Its flowers vary in color from yellow to orange to pink or red; infrequently they are white with yellow centers. It is a low shrub with a thick, strong wood.

A small, pretty, yellow-green bird, the anianiau (*Loxops*

parva), is common in the high forests of Kauai. It is difficult for the less-than-expert to tell the difference between the anianiau and the amakihi (*Loxops virents*), which is the same size and yellow. However, if you get a close look, the amakihi has a dark loral (space between the eye and bill) mark that joins the eye and the curved dark bill. No matter, for they are both pretty birds.

From the falls, the trail makes a steep climb out of the gulch and ascends the pali, from which some of the best vistas of Waimea are had. Once again, be careful, for while the trail is broad and easy to follow, steep walls drop to the canyon below. There are numerous places to pause in some shade to enjoy the view through the canyon to the sea on the south side.

After a steep climb, the trail ends at Kumuwela Lookout, from where you can return on the Canyon Trail or connect with the Kumuwela Road or the Ditch Trail.

Cliff Trail, .1 mile, 10 minutes (hike rating: family).
Park HQ to trailhead 2.1 miles.

The Cliff Trail provides a scenic vista of Waimea Canyon and a necessary departure point for the Canyon Trail. It begins after a short walk or drive down Halemanu Road.

Ditch Trail, 3.5 miles, 4 hours (hike rating: strenuous).
Park HQ to trailhead 1.7 miles.

The Ditch Trail is an ambitious hike over some very rough terrain. You can use the trail as part of a loop that also uses the Canyon Trail, or you can enter it from Kumuwela, Wainininua or Mohihi Road. In any event, the trail follows a circuitous route along a cliff and in and out of numerous gulches and small stream canyons.

The trail offers spectacular sights of the interior of Waimea, the broadest and deepest of the canyons. Across the canyon you'll see Kohua Ridge, with its many falls and cascades during rainy periods. Awini ("sharp, bold, forward") Falls is at the southwest tip of the ridge, with Mohihi Falls to the right-rear of the canyon and Moeloa ("to oversleep") Falls to the left-rear of the canyon.

The trail is rich with flora, from the common guava to lehua and a variety of ferns. The variety of tree fern (*Cibotium menziesii*) seen here is the "monkey's tail" fern, with its wiry black hairs on the frond stems. It has the biggest trunk of all Hawaiian tree ferns, a trunk often used for carving akuas (idols) or tikis.

Iliau Nature Loop, .3 mile, ¼ hour (hike rating: family). Park HQ to trailhead 6.3 miles.

The nature loop is a good place to see some 20 endemic plants, most of which are identified by name plates. The main attraction is the rare and unique iliau plant. The trail provides a number of vistas for viewing the Waimea canyon and Waialae (lit., "mudhen water") Falls on the opposite, east wall of the canyon.

Kaluapuhi Trail, 1.7 miles, 1½ hours (hike rating: hardy family). Park HQ to trailhead 1.9 miles.

Kaluapuhi (lit., "the eel pit") Trail is a favorite during plum season. If it is a good year (every second year, it seems) for the delicious Methley plum, this trail will take you to some of the best trees. The pickings are generally good due to the fact that the only access to the trees is on foot.

Plum picking is regulated by the state and is limited to 25 pounds of the fruit per person per day. Pickers must check in and out at the checking station, usually located near park headquarters. Many local people bring the whole family and sleep in their cars overnight near the station to get an early start in the morning. A favorite trick of locals is to tout visitors away from the best trees by advising them that they will find the sweetest plums somewhere else.

Access to the trail is a few feet off the main highway where a trail marker identifies the trailhead.

Koaie Canyon Trail, 3 miles, 2 hours (hike rating: difficult). In Waimea Canyon.

Koaie Canyon is a favorite of hikers and backpackers,

for its trail is easier than the Waimea Canyon Trail and it leads to a secluded wilderness shelter. The canyon's name comes from the koaie (*Acacia koaia*) tree, which is endemic to the islands and is much like the koa tree. The wood, however, is harder than koa wood, and was once used to make spears and fancy paddles.

To reach the trailhead, hike north along the Waimea River from the point where the Kukui Trail reaches the river. After .5 mile you reach the river crossing just below Poo Kaeha, a prominent hill about 500 feet above the river. Before crossing, look across the river to see if the ledge at the base of the cliff is visible. Unless it is, the river is too high and not safe to cross. Once across the river follow the ledge a short distance north to Koaie Stream. Follow the trail along the south side of the stream into Koaie Canyon.

The canyon is a fertile area that was once extensively farmed, as is evidenced by the many terraced areas you'll observe and the rock walls and the remains of house sites. You can usually find ample pools in the stream to swim in or at least to cool off in. During the summer months, the water is quite low, but usually sufficient for some relief from the hot canyon. The Division of Forestry is planning to open a number of wildland campsites in Koaie over the next few years. Presently, at trail's end, you'll find Lonomea Camp, an open shelter with table alongside the stream near a generous pool for swimming. The Lonomea (*Sapindus cahuensis*) is a native tree with ovate leaves which reaches heights of up to 30 feet. It grows only on Kauai and Oahu.

Don't forget to pack out your garbage.

Kukui Trail, 2.5 miles, loop, 2 hours (hike rating: strenuous). Elevation loss 2000 feet.

Park HQ to trailhead 6.3 miles.

The Kukui (candlenut lamp) Trail is the short route into Waimea Canyon. A Division of Forestry sign marks the departure point just off the Iliau trail (see its trail description above). Sign in (and out) on the trail register located near the trail's beginning. You may hike and camp in the canyon for 3 nights.

Kauai—Wailua Falls

Maui—Sliding Sands trail in Haleakala crater

Mountain apples

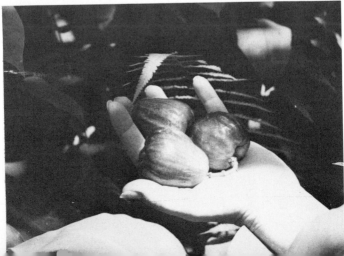

Oahu—99 steps on Diamond Head trail

Oahu—Manoa Falls trail

Maui—pool beside Hana road

Ti

Oahu—Toilet Bowl at Hanauma Bay

Maui—Haleakala crater

Kahali ginger

Bananas

The first part of the trail, dropping over 2000 feet into the canyon, is maintained. Beyond the midpoint, however, the trail is wet and overgrown, and some caution should be exercised. You may have to search out the trail. When in doubt stay out of the heavy growth and bear right.

You'll probably find numerous half-gallon plastic jugs along the trail. They are left by pig and goat hunters as they descend so they will have fresh water on their return. You should stay out of the brush so that you won't be mistaken for a goat or pig by hunters.

The first part of the hike offers some spectacular views of Waimea Canyon and Waialae Falls across the canyon on the east wall. The second part of the hike passes through heavy growth until it emerges at Wiliwili (a native tree bearing red seeds) Camp. Camp along the boulder-laden banks of Waimea River. It is a delightful spot to camp in shade with ample water from the stream. The water, however, should be boiled or otherwise treated for safety. Many hikers make a base camp at Wiliwili and then hike on the canyon trails and in the side canyons. If you are in good shape, it is possible to make the hike in and out in one day.

Waialae Canyon Trail, .3 mile, ½ hour (hike rating: strenuous).
In Waimea Canyon.

This short, undeveloped trail takes you south along Waimea River from the campground at the end of the Kukui Trail. A trail sign identifies the point where you can ford the river and enter lower Waialae Canyon. The trail follows the north side of Waialae Stream for a short distance to "Poachers Camp," to a shelter, table, and pit toilets.

Waimea Canyon Trail, 1.5 miles, 2 hours (hike rating: strenuous).
In Waimea Canyon.

The Waimea Canyon Trail travels north through the heart of the canyon to the junction of Koaie Stream and Waimea River. Well-maintained, it leads up the river on the west side to a point where a plantation ditchman's house is located. The trail was originally constructed for access to the canyon to construct and maintain a powerhouse up-river.

You reach the trail by hiking down the Kukui trail to the river, or by hiking seven miles up-river from Waimea town. The latter not only requires permission from a number of private parties but is a hot, exhausting trek. The Waimea Canyon trail also provides access to the Koaie and Kaluahaulu trails and to the inner recesses of the canyon.

Alakai Swamp Trail, 3.4 miles, 3 hours (hike rating: strenuous).
    Park HQ to trailhead 3.2 miles.
    Few will disagree that the Alakai (lit., "to lead") Swamp is the most interesting and exciting place on the island. For interest, there is the beautiful mokihana berry—Kauai's flower—and the native rainforests; and for excitement, there is the swamp with its bogs, where a false step puts you knee-deep in mud and water. Be prepared with strong hiking shoes.

The trailhead is at a forest-reserve marker beside Mohihi (Camp 10) Road, which cannot be traversed by a passenger car. (An alternative route is via the Pihea trail—see below). The trail follows a pole line constructed during World War II for Army communications. The trail is well-maintained and easy to follow, as the abandoned poles mark the way.

The first bog is near the one-mile marker. After the Alakai-Pihea Trail junction, which is identified by a trail sign, bogs become more frequent, wetter and deeper until the 2½-mile marker, from where it is all bog until trail's end. Your nose will be your guide to the mokihana (*Pelea anisata*) tree, which emits a strong anise odor. It is a small tree whose small berries are strung and worn in leis. Native to the islands, the mokihana berry is frequently twined with the maile vine to make a popular wedding lei. The maile (*Alyxia olivaeformis*) vine is common along the trail, with its tiny, glossy leaves and tiny, white flowers. Unlike the mokihana tree, the maile vine must be cut or its bark stripped before its musky, woodsy scent of anise is noticed.

After the first two miles of ascending and descending a number of small, fern-laden gulches, the broad, flat expanse of the swamp lies before you. There is little chance of getting off the trail if you follow the pole line, although you may have to circle here and there to avoid the wetter, deeper bogs. At the 2-3/4 mile marker you must make a left turn, leaving the pole line to follow white and brown pipe markers. With alertness and caution, you'll find your way.

At Kilohana ("lookout point" or "superior") Lookout, one has a magnificent view into Wainiha (lit., "unfriendly water") Valley, which extends from the sea to the base of Mt. Waialeale. Beyond Wainiha lies Hanalei (lit.,"crescent bay") with its conspicuous wide, deep bay. It's an enchanting place to picnic, rest and reflect.

Awaawapuhi Trail, 3.3 miles, 3 hours (hike rating: strenuous). Elevation loss 1600 feet.
   Park HQ to trailhead, 1.5 miles.
Of the number of trails that extend to points high above the Na Pali Coast and the extraordinarily beautiful valleys of the north shore, this is the best. You should be in good physical condition before attempting this hike, and be prepared with food, first-aid kit, sound hiking boots, and one quart of water per person. The rewards are great, as you pass through tropical forests to view the extremely precipitous and verdant valleys of Awaawapuhi (lit., "ginger valley") and Nualolo.

The trail begins north of Highway 55 at telephone pole No. 1-4/2 P/152, about halfway between the Kokee Museum and the Kalalau lookout. There is a forestry trail marker at the trailhead. The trail is well-maintained, and numerous markers show the way. You may make a 7-mile loop by returning via the Nualolo Trail.

The trail descends gradually through a moist native forest which becomes drier scrub as it reaches the ridges above the valley. You are most likely to see feral goats in the pali area. With binoculars you can watch goats forage while you picnic on any one of a number of overlooks about 2500

feet above the valley. Additionally, you will probably sight
helicopters flying tourists in, out, and over the pali, since the
Na Pali Coast is a favorite even of those who are unable or
unwilling to make the trip on foot.

At the 3-mile point, a trail marker identifies the Nualolo
Trail. The Nualolo Trail is in good condition and is a part of a
delightful loop hike which emerges 3.7 miles away on the
main road between the ranger's house and the housekeeping
cabins.

The Awaawapuhi Trail continues for 0.3 mile from the
junction to a vertical perch above the Na Pali Coast. This is
the best place to lunch and to watch goats. In over a dozen
visits to this promentory in recent years, I have seen goats
each time. It is a startling and exciting place.

**Honopu Trail, 2.5 miles, 2½ hours (hike rating: stren-
uous). Elevation loss 1500 feet.**
    Park HQ to trailhead 2.0 miles.
Like the Nualolo and the Awaawapuhi trails, this one
reaches excellent points from which to view the Na Pali
Coast. The Honopu (lit., "conch bay") Trail is not as well-
maintained as the others, and dangerous in places where
slides make passage along the pali difficult.

The trail begins about ½ mile past the trailhead for the
Awaawapuhi Trail north off Highway 55 and snakes along a
ridge through dry, forested areas and then through scrub
forests typical of the region. At numerous points you can
picnic and look deep into Honopu Valley, the so-called
"Valley of the Lost Tribe," where the remains of an ancient
Polynesian village have created a mystery as to who were
these people and what happened to them.

**Kawaikoi Stream Trail, 2.5 miles (loop), 1½ hours (hike
rating: hardy family).**
    Park HQ to trailhead 3.8 miles.
Access to the Kawaikoi (lit., "the flowing water") Stream
Trail is off the Mohihi (Camp 10) Road, which is passable
only in a four-wheel-drive vehicle. A 2½-mile loop-trail hike
was made possible in 1975 when the Forest Service and the

Hawaii Chapter of the Sierra Club connected the Kawaikoi Trail with the Pihea Trail.

The route begins opposite a planted forest of Japanese sugi pines and follows the south side of Kawaikoi Stream along an easy, well-defined trail in heavy vegetation. During rainy periods, this is a muddy trail. A short distance past the 0.5 mile point, a trail sign indicates a place to cross the stream to join the Pihea Trail on the north side of the stream. If the rocks are not visible, then the water is too high for a safe crossing. The Kawaikoi Trail itself continues east on the south side of the stream to 100 yards past the ¾-mile marker, where a trail sign marks the loop portion of the route. During the 1-mile loop it is necessary to cross the stream twice.

In recent years, there has been a good deal of grass planting and herbicide work in the area in an effort to control blackberry, which is threatening to take over not only this area but also a number of other areas in the park.

There are many swimming holes in this generous stream and places along the bank to spend some peaceful moments. You may agree with Ralph Daehler, District Forester, who stated that Kawaikoi is the most beautiful place on Kauai.

Nualolo Trail, 3.7 miles, 3 hours (hike rating: strenuous). Elevation loss 1500 feet.
50 yards west of Park HQ.

This is the third and the easiest of the three trails to the Na Pali Coast. The trail starts between the ranger station and the housekeeping cabins in Kokee, and combined with the Awaawaphui Trail makes a 7-mile loop hike (add 1.5 miles if you must hike the highway from the Awaawapuhi Trailhead to the ranger station).

The first part of the trail passes through a native forest of tall trees for a pleasant, cool hike. The trail then descends about 1500 feet to a number of viewpoints overlooking Nualolo Valley. Feral goats, common along the cliffs, can be found foraging in cool, shady places. Carry water and food, for neither is available.

At the 2-mile marker, the Lolo Bench Mark Trail goes

left for about one mile. It is a little used trail that only goat hunters follow. From this junction the Nualolo Trail goes right and begins to make a more abrupt descent over some badly eroded places where only the sure-footed should pass. Be cautious, for a fall could result in serious injury. A second junction is reached at the 2½-mile marker. The trail to the left here goes to the Lolo Bench Mark vista. Continue to the right a short distance to the first of a number of viewpoints of Nualolo Valley from places about 2800 feet above the valley. At the 3-3/4 mile point the Nualolo Trail ends where it joins the Awaawapuhi Trail. At this junction the Awaawapuhi Trail goes left 0.3-mile to a superb viewpoint and right 3 miles to the main highway.

**Pihea Trail, 3.3 miles, 3 hours (hike rating: strenuous).
Park HQ to trailhead 3.8 miles.**

Pihea ("din of voices crying, shouting, wailing, lamentation") Trail is the newest trail—the last 1½ miles were completed in 1975—in the Kokee area. It begins at the end of the highway, 3.6 miles from the campground, at Puu O Kila (lit., "Kila's Hill"), overlooking Kalalau Valley. The first 3/4 mile follows the remains of a county road project which was begun in a cloud of controversy and which terminated literally in the mire when money ran out, along with the willingness to continue. A road through the Alakai Swamp and down the mountain to Hanalei would have been a great tourist attraction and an engineering feat, but an ecological disaster.

From the lookout you can usually see the white-tailed tropic bird (*Phaethon lepturus*) soaring along the cliffs of Kalalau Valley. This bird is white with large black wing patches above and 16-inch white tail streamers. A similar bird that is all white except for red tail streamers is the red-tailed tropic-bird (*Phaethon rubricauda*).

After enjoying the breathtaking views into Kalalau, your trail follows the rim of the valley to Pihea, the last overlook into Kalalau before the Alakai Swamp. The trail makes an abrupt right turn as it enters the swamp and then drops in and out of a number of gulches to the junction (posted) with the Alakai Swamp Trail.

The Pihea Trail can be used as part of a shuttle trip from Kalalau Lookout into the Alakai Swamp, with a return to park headquarters via the Alakai Swamp Trail or the Kawaikoi Stream Trail and the Camp 10 Road.

Both the maile vine and the mokihana tree (see the Alakai Swamp Trail for description) are common along the trail and are favorites of both locals and visitors. The mokihana's powerful anise aroma attracts immediate attention.

Also common in this area is the ohia lehua (*Metrosideros collina*), with its tufted red stamens that remind the visitor of the mainland bottlebrush tree. A variety of tree ferns abound along the trail, the hapu'u (*Cibotium chamissoi*) and the amaumau (*Sadleria cyatheoides*) being most common. The latter grows to 10 feet in height. Its pinnate fronds were once used for huts, and the juice from it for a reddish dye.

From the junction with the Alakai Swamp Trail, our trail continues over the newest portion, passing through native forests, crossing small streams, and winding through verdant gulches until it reaches the north bank of Kawaikoi Stream. You can stay on the north side of the stream and follow the trail 0.5 mile to Camp 10 Road, or at a sign by the stream it is possible to rock-hop across the stream and to follow the Kawaikoi Trail west for 0.5 mile to Camp 10 Road. Do not cross the stream if the water is too high. The Pihea Trail, on the north side of the stream, is usually drier.

98

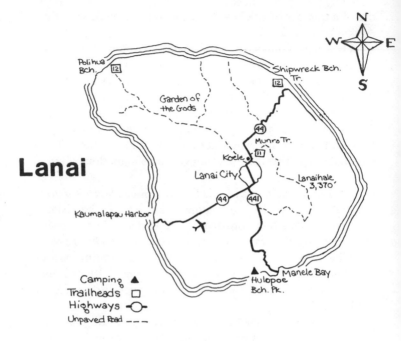

Lanai

The Island

Lanai may be small—just 17 miles long and 13 miles wide—it may not have adequate visitor accommodations, and it may not have many hiking trails, but it does have one of the best swimming, camping, and snorkeling beaches anywhere. Hulopoe Beach is a dream place to "kick back" and a good basecamp from which to explore the island. Lanai is mostly owned by the Dole Pineapple Co. (Castle & Cook, Inc.) which cultivates pineapple on about 16 percent of the island.

Although Lanai is known quite properly as the "Pineapple Island" today, its past belies this innocent nickname. Historically, Lanai was a place where *kapu* (taboo) violators were banished and where life was once difficult on this wild, arid land (42 inches of rainfall in the center of the island). Additionally, the aliis (chiefs) frequently brought their dead to Lanai to be buried. Consequently, legends abound regarding ghosts who inhabit the island today. One legend tells of Kaululaau, who for his evil deeds was exiled by his uncle, the king of Maui. Kaululaau is thought to have made Lanai safe for human habitation by fighting the ghosts and driving off the evil spirits.

Today, this tiny island, which was created by a single crater volcano, Palawai, is not a modern tourist-oriented Pacific island by any stretch of the imagination. Castle and Cook have plans to develop the island on a "controlled" basis to attract tourists. Meanwhile, Lanai remains a peaceful stopover for the person who can do without luxury. Lanai City is in the center of the island in the foothills of a small mountain range that is topped by Lanaihale (3370 ft.), the highest place on the island. Politically, the 2200 residents are part of Maui County. The island has one 11-room hotel, a couple of grocery stores, a snack shop, and the usual assortment of government buildings. That's it! There are no restaurants (one small dining room in the hotel, with limited menu and hours) no shopping centers, no gift shops, no bars, no nightclubs, and no public transportation. Why would they need public transportation? There are no public roads to speak of. The "paved" roads are narrow and in poor condition. Consequently, although expensive to rent, a jeep is advisable to travel the pineapple and mountain roads. However, local people are friendly, so that rides are not difficult to get on the main roads.

Camping

Hulopoe Beach is outstanding for camping. The only drawback is that it is very expensive by Hawaiian standards and even mainland standards. The campground is privately owned by the Kiele Company. There is a $5.00 (1981) one-time registration fee and a $3.80 (1981) fee per day per person regardless of age. Reservations and applications should be made at least one week in advance, since there are only six (6) campsites in a shaded Kiawe-tree area and the stay is limited to seven days. When I camped at Hulopoe in July 1981 for four nights over a weekend, there were no other campers until the last night, when a group of teenagers from Oahu set up a camp. There are clean restrooms, fire pits, tables and showers. The latter are "cold water." However, apparently the pipes are so close to the ground surface that the sun heats the water. Be certain to bring snorkeling equipment, for there are few places to compare with Hulopoe.

Hiking

There are four notable hikes on the island—one beach hike and three in the mountain range above Lanai City. With the exception of the Munro Trail, there is no backpacking experience. Most of the island is flat, with a modest cluster of hills above Lanai City. A major considera-tion is that most of the trailheads are accessible only by jeep.

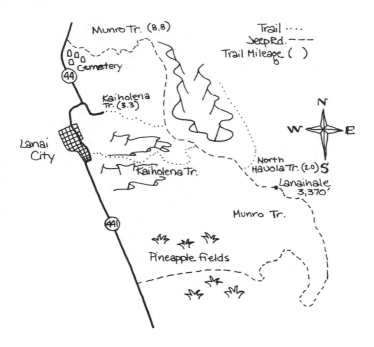

11 Munro Trail Hikes

Rating: See individual hikes.

Features: Viewpoints, fruits, Lanai's highest point—Lanaihale, 3370 feet.

Permission: None.

Hiking Distance & Time: See individual hikes.

Introductory Notes: Do not attempt to drive a conventional vehicle on the Munro Trail. It begins innocently, but it soon becomes wet and rutted. It is possible to travel the entire trail in a four wheel-drive vehicle. George C. Munro, after whom the trail is named, was a naturalist who is credited with reforesting this part of Lanai with exotic tropicals in an effort to restore a watershed area.

Munro Trail, 8.8 miles one-way, 8 hours (hike rating: strenuous). Elevation gain 1400 feet.

Driving Instructions:

2.4 miles, ¼ hr. From the Post Office on Lanai Ave. drive north on Route 44 to the end of town and bear right on Keomuku Road. Two miles from the Post Office, turn right on a paved-graveled road and drive 0.4 mile past a cemetery on the right to the trailhead.

On the Trail: From the trailhead, the jeep road-trail crosses a flat, grassy place. After 200 yards bear left at a junction with a faint road which bears right. The trail descends into Maunalei (lit., "lei mountain") Gulch, which is shaded for about a mile by large eucalyptus trees. Maunalei was so named because the clouds over the mountain suggest a lei. Edible thimbleberries (*Rubus rosaefolius*) are plentiful for the entire length of the trail. They grow on a small, thorny bush with white flowers. The trail begins an ascent on the east side of the mountains, from which views of Maui (east) and Molokai (northeast) are possible. At the head of Manalei Gulch (southeast) is the place where in 1778 the king of Hawaii massacred many Lanai natives who sought shelter in this stronghold. Beyond the gulch, the trail passes alternately through open areas and forested areas in which Norfolk Island pines (*Araucaria excelsa*) dominate. These tall, perfectly symmetrical trees were chosen by Munro and others to increase Lanai's ground water, since the trees collect moisture from low-hanging clouds. After a steep climb along the east side of the range, the trail reaches some flat areas. At 3.6 miles a spur road turns right onto a small clearing, on which you will find an abandoned rain gauge and a house site. This road is part of the Kaiholena Gulch Trail (see map).

Along the upper Munro Trail there are numerous flat, grassy places to camp. Legally, you should get a permit to camp from the Department of Land and Natural Resources in Lanai City, but I doubt if anyone does. Just before the summit is reached, at 4.7 miles, a trail marker on the left identifies the North Hauola Trail (see trail description). Lanaihale (lit., "house of Lanai") is just beyond. At 5.3

miles look for a turnout on the right, a picnic table and a good spot to view Lanai City and the west side of the island. It is also a good place to camp, although it can be a bit wet. One-half mile beyond, a trail sign on the left identifies the East Hauola Trail. This is a little-used trail which is heavily overgrown and not as good a trail as North Hauola. The latter is a much more appealing hiking experience. From this junction the Munro trail makes an abrupt descent and from a number of clearings provides views of Maui (east), Kahoolawe (southeast) and Hawaii beyond on a clear day. The trail ends when you reach the pineapple fields. Stay on the main roads (24 feet wide) bearing to the right to reach Lanai City.

North Hauola Trail, 2 miles one-way, 1½ hours (hike rating: strenuous). Elevation gain 1500 feet. (For driving instructions see the previous trail.)

Introductory Notes: I suggest North Hauola as a side hike off the Munro Trail as far as the eucalyptus grove and back. This is the prettiest part of the trail.

On the Trail: From the outset ferns, thimbleberries and a variety of scrub partly obstruct the trail, so that long pants are advised to avoid scratches. The first mile of the trail is quite wet, with a lot of muddy places and mudholes to challenge the hiker's agility. The trail follows the crest of a ridge, which is dominated by Norfolk Island pines. With clear weather, you should be able to see (from left to right) Oahu (far to the northwest) Molokai, Maui, Kahoolawe and sometimes, Hawaii (far to the southeast). Additionally, there are some dramatic views into Maunalei Gulch on the left and Hauola Gulch on the right. Use caution if you walk to the edge of the ridge, for the walls on both sides are nearly vertical. For my taste, the interesting and beautiful part of the hike is to the eucalyptus grove. From there I recommend that you retrace your steps and continue on the Munro Trail. If you continue to the coast, you should continue through the grove and follow a ridge to the right, which will lead you to a point overlooking Maunalei Gulch (left) and the Koolanai jeep road, which will take you to the coast.

Kaiholena Gulch Trail, 3.3 miles one-way, 2 hours (hike rating: strenuous). Elevation gain 1050 feet.

Driving Instructions: (1.5 miles) From the Post Office on Lanai Ave. drive north on Route 44 to the end of town and bear right on Keomuku Road. Take a right on a dirt road between a park pavillion (left) and a golf course (right). Take the first left, bear right past two roads to the left, and go left up a small rise toward a grove of Norfolk Island pines. Park just before the pines in a turnout (right) by a telephone pole. This is the trailhead.

Introductory Notes: Kaiholena (iholena is a type of banana) Gulch is a pleasant mountain hike which provides some outstanding views of the west side of Lanai. It could also serve as a shortcut to the Munro Trail, which it joins at the 3.1 mile point of the latter.

On the Trail: The trail follows the poleline up the hill and passes through the twin poles at the top of the rise. It then swings right, into a grove of eucalyptus trees, and begins an ascent on a ridge between Kaiholena Gulch on the right and Hulopoe (named after a man) Gulch on the left. The trail is in good condition and easy to follow to the Munro trail-road about one mile distant. Throughout the hike, but particularly on the higher parts, be on the lookout for ripe common and strawberry guavas. The former are soft, yellow and lemon-sized when ripe, and the latter are crimson and cherry-to-plum-sized when ripe. Both can be quite sweet and both are high in vitamin C. The tall trees that dominate the first part of the trail are all introduced trees, the result of reforestation programs. Eucalyptus (many species), Norfolk Island Pine and ironwood are abundant here and throughout Hawaii. The ironwood, with its long, slender, drooping, dull-green needles, makes a good windbreak and the fallen needles make a soft mat for a camper.

After one mile the trail meets the Muntro trail-road, and we turn right onto it. Views of the west side of Maui are possible along the road, which is bordered with Norfolk Island and sugi pines. Walk southeast along the road for about ½ mile until you come to a vehicle turnout on the right and a small clearing on which you will see an abandoned rain gauge and a housesite. All that remains of the house site is a set of stairs which lead dangerously into a gulch. From the "staircase" and the abandoned housesite, the trail goes northwest, then shortly turns south to a flat area. This section was marked with trail tape in 1981 and was easy to follow, although staghorn ferns and the thimbleberry bushes with their thorns reached across the trail in many places. The result was a lot of scratches if you were wearing shorts. Along the trail on the flats, there are a couple of short spur trails which lead to the left to lookouts into the gulch below. Be cautious at these vista points for they are at the tops of nearly vertical walls.

The trail continues up the ridge to its highest point, Puu Alii (lit., "royal hill") from which views of Lanai City are good. The northwestward descent from the hill is at first gradual, but then you reach a steep, eroded area and the rest of the descent is more abrupt. Molokai should be visible to your front right. The section of trail to the pineapple fields should be clear and in good condition since locals hike or ride horses over it. Continue into a eucalyptus grove for a short distance to where the trail turns sharply left and follow a relatively steep and eroded ridgeline to a large communications reflector and to the pineapple fields a short distance beyond. Once on the pineapple road, follow the shortest route to Lanai City, which is clearly distinguishable about one mile distant, or, if you wish to return to the trailhead, follow the pineapple roads north to a cluster of Norfolk Island pines about 1½ miles away.

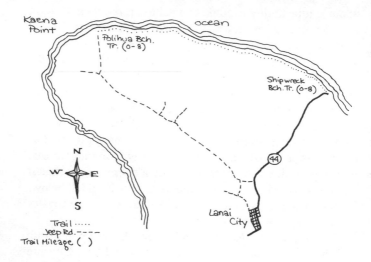

Kaena Point

ocean

Polihua Bch.
Tr. (0-8)

Shipwreck
Bch.Tr. (0-8)

N
W　　E
S

44

Lanai
City

Trail ·····
Jeep Rd. - - - -
Trail Mileage ( )

12　Shipwreck Beach

Rating: Family to strenuous

Features: Shipwrecks, beachcombing for wreckage, shells, glass floats.

Permission: None.

Hiking Distance & Time: 0-8 miles one-way, ½ hour per mile.

Driving Instructions to Shipwreck Beach: 10.3 miles, 1 hour. From the Post Office on Lanai Ave. drive north on Route 44 to the end of town, bear right on Keomuku Road and drive to the end of the paved road. Turn left on a dirt-sand road and go 1.8 miles, which is as far as even a jeep can travel.

Introductory Notes: The 8 miles between Shipwreck Beach and Polihua Beach are a long, hot hike, but not without rewards. The entire length of the beach along the north-northeast shore of Lanai is littered with shipwreckage, seashells, and a variety of ocean debris. It is certainly a beachcomber's delight; the pickings are good on this little-traveled beach. If you take the entire hike, transportation is a problem unless you retrace your steps. Certainly, the one-mile hike to the largest shipwreck on the coast is worth the hike.

On the Trail: The trail begins on a rocky ledge above the water at Kukui (lit., "candlenut lamp") Point, once the site of a lighthouse. All that remains of the lighthouse is a large concrete slab. The interesting beach houses near the point are almost entirely constructed of timbers from ships and an assortment of driftwood. The trail-beachfront is only a few yards wide even at low tide, and the rotting timbers of ships tend to block your passage. It is fun to examine the wreckage and to splash in the shallow water for relief from the heat. There is no good swimming beach, for the surf bottom here is largely rough lava, and beach stones. However, it is a good fishing area where locals may be observed pole fishing or throwing a net a hundred yards offshore, since it is so shallow. From Kukui Point to a place opposite the rusting hulk of a large ship about 150 yards offshore is one mile.

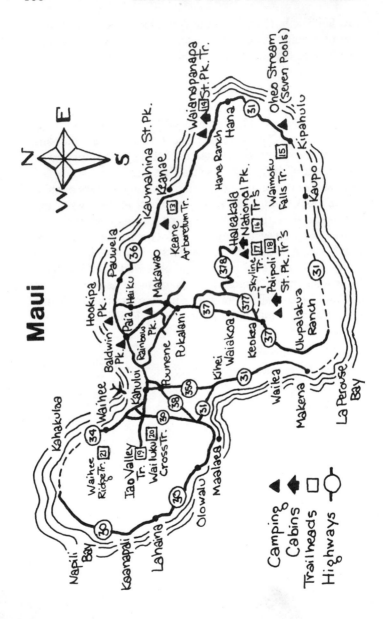

Maui

The Island

Adventurers come in all shapes, sizes and dispositions. Some enjoy the challenge of trudging through a quagmire in wind and rain in order to stand atop a mountain whose name is unknown to most people. Others find wonder in a crater conformed like the surface of the moon, with no familiar sights or sounds except the sounds made by the wind. Still others prefer a leisurely walk to a fern-rimmed pool and a cool swim beneath a waterfall.

All these options are possible within 729 square miles in a land of contrasts, in a land of unmatched beauty, in a land often equated with paradise by the casual visitor as well as the native-born. It's the Valley Isle—Maui. As the familiar stenciled T-shirt proclaims, "Maui No Ka Oi"—"Maui is the best." Maui has 150 miles of coastline, with 33 miles suitable for swimming. The Valley Isle possesses more beach area than any other Hawaiian island, which probably accounts for its exceptional popularity.

The island of Maui is the result of eruptions of two large volcanoes, which first formed separate land masses that were later joined by succeeding eruptions. Although some debate exists over the origin of the name, many people believe the island was named after Maui, a legendary superman, who lassoed the sun to bring daylight to the island. In spite of this male giant's influence, locals refer to Maui as "our beautiful lady" because of the island's curvaceous physical appearance. Topped by 10,023-foot Haleakala, the lady's skirt fans out in multitudinous pleats in the form of valleys and gulches. Some are usually dry, awaiting the seasonal rains. Others are usually wet and abound with introduced and native flora and fauna.

Camping

Campgrounds and state rental cabins on Maui range from adequate to good and contain most of the amenities. Fees are modest and assure an inexpensive stay on the island. The map above locates the county, state and national campgrounds, camping shelters, and cabins.

The county of Maui provides three tent and mobile (auto camper) campgrounds. Two camping areas are located on the north shore: H.A. Baldwin Park is 10 miles from Wailuku, and Hookipa Beach Park is 15 miles from Wailuku. The latter is regarded by surfers as one of the finest surfing areas in the Hawaiian chain. Rainbow Park, 12 miles from Wailuku, is not recommended because of its remote location and poor facilities. Permits are required in county parks and are limited to 3 days per year. Camping fees are $3 for adults and $.50 for persons under 18. Each park except Rainbow has water, tables, restrooms, outdoor showers and grills. For reservations, write the Maui Department of Parks and Recreation. (All addresses are in the appendix.)

The State of Hawaii provides three campgrounds. Two are located on the east side of the island. Kaumahina State Wayside Park is 30 miles from Wailuku, and Waianapanapa State Park is 51 miles from there. Both parks are in beautiful settings. The former is on a cliff overlooking the east coast, while the latter is on a bluff overlooking a black-sand beach. If you are looking for solitude, the third state campground, at Polipoli State Park, will satisfy you. Polipoli is 31 miles from Wailuku, in Maui's upcountry at 6200 feet elevation. The maximum length of stay is 5 nights. There is no fee for any state park, but a permit is required.

In addition to the campgrounds, the State of Hawaii also operates rental cabins at two locations. Each of the 12 cabins at Waianapanapa accommodates up to 6 people and is completely furnished with bedding, towels, cooking and eating utensils, electricity, hot water, showers, electric stoves and refrigerators. The one Polipoli cabin has similar facilities except that it has no electricity and has a gas stove and a cold shower only. The Polipoli cabin accommodates up to 10 persons. The cabins at both locations are comfortable and inexpensive. The maximum cost at Waianapanapa per cabin per day is $30 and at Polipoli is $50. For reservations or permits for the cabins and campgrounds, write or contact the Division of State Parks.

The National Park Service operates campgrounds and rental cabins in Haleakala National Park. One campground is located outside the crater at Hosmer Grove, a short walk from park headquarters at 7000 feet. Two other campgrounds are located in the crater—at Paliku Cabin on the east side and at Holua Cabin on the north side. Wilderness permits are required only for the crater campgrounds, where tenting is limited to three nights and four days. Tenting is limited to two nights at one site. Tenting is further limited to 50 persons per day, with 25 only per camping site. There is no fee for any of the campgrounds. The campgrounds are rarely full. There is one other campground in the park, located at sea level in the Kipahulu (formerly Seven Sacred Pools) section of the park. It is a primitive camping area without water. Permits are available at park headquarters.

Use of the crater cabins presents a definite problem because of their popularity with visitors and locals. There are three cabins available in the crater—at Paliku, at Holua and at Kapalaoa (see the Haleakala map). Each cabin is equipped with water, pit toilet, wood-burning cook stove, firewood, cooking and eating utensils, 12 bunks, mattresses and blankets (pillows and sheets are not supplied). You must bring a warm sleeping bag. Use is limited to 12 persons per group, and, as with tenting, limited to three nights—two nights at any one site. Rates are $5 per night and $2.50 for children under 13, with a $15 nightly minimum. A lottery is conducted to determine cabin users. To participate, you must write to the Superintendent, Haleakala National Park, at least 90 days in advance, giving an outline of your proposed trip, including the number in your group, the exact dates and which cabin you want to use each night. You will be contacted only if your request is drawn. Don't pass up hiking and camping in Haleakala. It is one of the best places for both in the islands.

The Maui Land & Pineapple Company allows camping by permission (tel. 669-6201) on their property at Windmill Beach, which is 16 miles north of Lahaina. Windmill is a good swimming and snorkeling beach, but there is no water and no facilities.

Hiking

Maui is not only the second largest of the Hawaiian Islands in size (Hawaii is the largest) but also the second most visited. More and more tourists are departing from the tour-bus route and becoming familiar with a Maui previously known only to natives. Campers, bicyclists and hikers are now more numerous and visible. There are hikes on Maui to satisfy the tenderfoot at well as the backpacker—short, easy hikes for the family, which reveal the beauty of the valleys, and more strenuous hikes, which do not necessarily reveal more but which fulfill the spirit of the more adventurous.

The island provides a great variety of hiking experiences. the verdant coastline and the valleys on the east side contain some fine hiking trails and places to find solitude. Haleakala National Park, particularly Haleakala Crater, has some outstanding hiking trails which provide the hiker with unique experiences. Hike Maui for a week or two and you too will say, "Maui No Ka Oi."

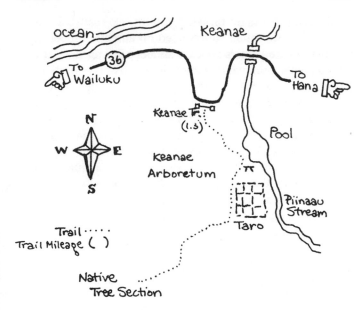

13   Keanae Arboretum

Rating: Hardy family.

Features: Swimming, fruits and native flora (identified).

Permission: None.

Hiking Distance & Time: 1.3 miles, 1½ hours.

Driving Instructions:

>*From Lahaina* (53 miles, 2 hours) southeast on Route 30, right on Route 380, right on Route 36 to the arboretum.

>*From Wailuku* (34 miles, 1½ hours) east on Route 32, right on Route 36 to the arboretum.

Introductory Notes: Keanae (lit., "the mullet") Arboretum provides an excellent introduction to native and introduced plants in a setting much like old Hawaii. Three distinct sections feature cultivated Hawaiian plants, native forest trees, and introduced tropical trees. You can enjoy all this and a swim in a fresh-water pool.

On the Trail: From the turnstile, a short jeep road (0.2 mile) leads to the arboretum. Introduced ornamental timber and fruit trees located in this area are all identified for the visitor. The fruit of the pummelo (*Citrus macima*) tree is of particular interest and good taste. It is a large, melon-sized fruit that has the aroma and taste of both grapefruit and orange. There are numerous banana and papaya plants. The area features several patches of irrigated taro, representing many of the varieties planted by the Hawaiians. Poi, a native staple, is produced from the taro root. Picnicking is available and encouraged in the grove alongside Piinaau (lit., "climb, mount") Stream, which is an inviting place to swim.

At the far end of the domestic-plant section and taro patches, a trail (1 mile) leads to a large forested flat that is representative of a Hawaiian rain forest. The trail winds through some heavy growth in places and crosses the stream 10 times, offering some welcome relief from the heat. Bear left at the first stream crossing and follow the trail, which parallels the stream below. About 100 yards from the first stream crossing, you will find the best pools and even a few relatively smooth, short water slides.

From the pools, the trail is not marked and not always discernible. However, you are in a narrow canyon, so you should find your way without getting lost. If in doubt, turn back. The native tree grove is at trail's end on a large, flat, boggy area. Unfortunately, in March 1985, I could not find a single marker identifying the trees and plants.

Return to Piinaau Stream for lunch and a swim in the cool mountain water.

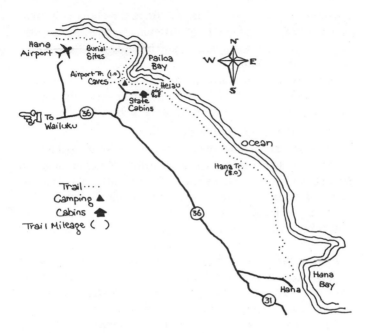

14 Waianapanapa State Park

Rating: Hardy Family.

Features: Lava flows and formations, heiaus, burial sites, swimming, camping, blowholes, caves, black-sand beach.

Permission: For camping reservations and permits write Division of State Parks.

Hiking Distance & Time: Consult individual hikes.

Driving Instructions:

From Lahaina (70 miles, 2½ hours) southeast on Route 30, right on Route 380, right on Route 36, left on road to Waianapanapa State Park.

From Wailuku (51 miles, 2 hours) east on Route 32, right on Route 36, then as above.

Introductory Notes: A round trip from Wailuku to Hana in one day is exhausting. To enjoy the beauty and serenity of the area, take a couple of days to drive the Hana Highway, camp at Waianapanapa (lit., "glistening water") State Park, swim at the black-sand beach, and hike the lava flows to the airport and to Hana.

Cabins situated along the beach are fully furnished and very comfortable. Each has beds, linen, utensils and an electric stove. All you need to bring is food.

North to the Airport, 1 mile, 1 hour.

The trail north from the black-sand beach is particularly rough because of the lava rocks underfoot. After passing two small bays, look for Hawaiian burial grounds and a heiau on your left where the terrain levels somewhat. The gravesites on top of the rough aa rock are rather prominent mounds. As you hike, you will be aware of the pounding surf and the interesting formations in the lava rock. Children enjoy assigning names to these strange forms. Be careful, as the trail is often precariously close to the surf. You are hiking over an early Hawaiian shoreline trail extending to the Piilanihale Heiau some three miles north of the airport.

You may choose to return to Waianapanapa via the shoreline route or to take the paved road by the airport to the Hana Highway and follow it to Waianapanapa for lunch.

South to Hana, 3 miles, 2 hours (trail rating: hardy family).

The trail south begins on a cliff above Pailoa (lit., "always splashing") Bay, with its black-sand beach, and follows the coastline—at times coming precariously close to the edge—to the enclosed bay at Hana.

Just below the campground you'll find burial sites decorated with artificial flowers overlooking a rather fragile lava formation. The lava flow is undoubtedly honeycombed with tunnels and caves, evidenced by the many pits and holes and by the sound of rushing, crashing surf underfoot. Indeed, one blowhole is just a few hundred feet beyond the burial grounds.

The white substance on the lava is called Hawaiian "snow." A lichen, it is the first plant to grow on fresh lava. Other plants along the hike include the hala (*Pandanus odoratissimus*), which produces a large, pineapple-shaped fruit. It is also called "tourist pineapple" since locals jokingly identify it as such to visitors. Beach morning glory (*Ipomoea pesca-prae*), with its pretty, delicate blue or purple flowers, plays an important role in preventing wind and water erosion of beaches by forming a large carpet. Also, a bush form of sandalwood (*Santalum ellipticum*), which grows less than three feet high, is rather profuse in most areas.

You'll find rental cabins nestled among the hala trees at 0.5 mile, with a number of trails leading from them to the beach. At 0.6 mile a small bridge crosses a natural arch in the lava under which the surf pounds and crashes as small crabs scurry about. Just before the bridge, you may be sprayed by a small blowhole that is particularly active when the surf is up.

Overlooking the sea from its volcanic perch (0.7 mile) is a heiau (a place of worship). Heiaus played an important part in pre-Christian Hawaiian culture. There are hundreds of known heiaus on the islands that served specifically to ensure rain, good crops, or success in war, while others were used for human sacrifice. Some people believe that if you wrap a stone in a leaf and place it on the walls of a heiau, you will be protected from harm. From the heiau, you pass a generous growth of hala, follow the coastline at its very edge, and reach a point about 50 feet above the surf. From here, about midpoint in the hike, you can see the cross on Mt. Lyons erected in memory of Paul Fagan, founder of the Hana Ranch and Hotel. You can also see tree-covered Kauiki (lit., "glimmer") Head, an imposing buttress on the south side of Hana Bay.

The trail is no longer clearly identifiable. However, you should not have any problem if you follow the coastline and avoid "ankle twisters" on the broken lava. You will find numerous caves and pits caused by gas that was trapped under the lava as the surface cooled. Later, the brittle surface collapsed, leaving some interesting holes.

When you arrive on a boulder-laden beach, a sign marks the trail's end. From here, you can take any of the roads leading to the Hana Highway for a return trip to Waiana-panapa, continue along the beach for ½ mile to Hana Bay, or return to the park via the lava flows. It is worth the extra hike to Hana Bay for lunch and a swim at its calm, gray-colored beach. The water at Hana Bay is not dirty but simply discolored by decomposed lava.

Before you leave Waianapanapa, be sure to take the short, ¼-mile hike to the caves, where it is possible to swim underwater to a chamber with a rock ledge. Legend recounts that a Hawaiian princess hid in the cave from her jealous husband, who, while resting by the cave, saw her reflection in the water. Since the ledge in the cave was a reputed meeting place for lovers, he promptly slew her by smashing her head against the walls of the cave. Consequently, it is said, the water in the pool turns blood-red every April, and her screams can be heard. If you cannot accept this legend, you may choose to believe that the red color of the water is the result of the tiny red shrimps that frequent the pool, and the "screams" are the result of the water and wind sweeping into the lava tube from the ocean.

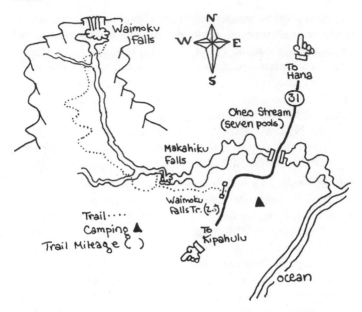

15   Waimoku Falls

Rating: Hardy Family.

Features: Waimoku Falls, bamboo forest, ancient Hawaiian agricultural sites, swimming, Oheo (formerly called Seven Sacred Pools), fruit, free camping.

Permission: None.

Hiking Distance & Time: 2.5 miles, 2 hours.

Driving Instructions:

From Lahaina (82 miles, 3½ hours) southeast on Route 30, right on Route 380, right on Route 36 to Hana, right on Route 31 to Oheo Stream.

From Wailuku (63 miles, 3 hours) east on Route 32, right on Route 36 to Hana, then as above.

Introductory Notes: The Hana Highway and the pools in Oheo ("something special") area (formerly Seven Sacred Pools) are two of the most popular tourist attractions on the island. To avoid a tiring return trip to central Maui the same day, you should consider staying at a hotel, camping near the pools in the national park, or staying at the cabins or campgrounds outside Hana at Waianapanapa State Park. The Park Service campground is located on pasture land south of the pools, on a bluff overlooking the rugged coastline. There is no water available. Chemical toilets are placed throughout the parking area.

The National Park Service rangers conduct a hike to Waimoku (lit., "flash flood") Falls every Saturday, departing from the Oheo Stream Bridge at 9 a.m. sharp.

On the Trail: The route begins opposite the parking lot on the south of the bridge, ascends through pasture land, and then parallels the stream below. A few hundred yards from the trailhead stands a 10-foot-tall concrete support, which is all that remains of a water-flume system that once spanned the stream and carried sugar cane to a now abandoned sugar mill one mile away in Kipahulu. The first highlight along the trail, however, is at the ½-mile point, where 184-foot Makahiku Falls drops into a stunning gorge below. To the left of the lookout, an abandoned irrigation ditch cut in the cliff allows you to hike to the top of the falls, a favorite of nude sun-worshippers. (Park rules prohibit nudity.) Be cautious as you walk in the ditch. You may encounter a cow, and there is not enough room for the both of you! Retrace your steps to the pasture land and to the trail to Waimoku.

While hiking through the pasture land, sample the gauvas. They were relatively sweet the last time I hiked to the falls. Grazing cattle do not seem disturbed by your presence in this pastoral setting. As you hike toward the mountains, a number of waterfalls are visible.

At the 1-mile point, a trail marker directs you into the woods and to the first stream crossing. As a sign notes, if the water is high in the stream and crossing is not easy, do not attempt to continue. At the stream crossing, there are several generous pools suitable for swimming. Don't be surprised to see some nude bathers doing just that. After the stream crossing and on to the falls, the trail is always wet and muddy. It is well-defined, but expect to make two more stream crossings, to hop over slippery rocks, and to carefully avoid the exposed roots on the trail. The Park Service recently placed some sections of boardwalk in the muddiest places.

The trail takes you through two marvelous bamboo forests. If the wind is up, you'll be serenaded by a discordant symphony of rattling bamboo. Beyond this "musical" forest are the remains of old taro patches, evidenced by walled terraces and shelter sites. Additionally, there are edible thimbleberries, coffee plants and, of course, guavas. With luck you will also find ripe mountain apples (*Eugenia malaccensis*) with small, deep-crimson fruit with a pure white pulp and a large round seed.

Shortly, Waimoku Falls comes into view. It's an idyllic spot to picnic after a pleasant hike. Before you shower under the falls, remember that most of the rocks in the stream fell from above!

16 Haleakala National Park (Crater)

Rating: Strenuous.

Features: "Moon" hiking, silversword, nene (a goose which is the Hawaiian state bird), lava tubes, lava formations, feral goats, camping.

Permission: Hiking and cabin permits from Haleakala National Park.

Hiking Distance & Time: See the mileage tables in the text below.

Driving Instructions:

> *From Lahaina* (59 miles, 2 hours) southeast on Route 30, right on Route 380, right on Route 36, right on Route 37, left on Route 377, left on Route 378 to the summit (Park Headquarters is 11 miles before the summit).

> *From Wailuku* (40 miles, 1½ hours) east on Route 32, right on Route 36, then as above.

As you drive to the summit of Haleakala look for the large (three-foot) ring-necked pheasant (*Phasianus colchicus torquatus*) and the smaller chukar (*Alectoris graeca*) with its brownish black markings and a black band extending through each eye and joining at the lower throat. Both flush along the road and may also be seen in the crater.

Introductory Notes: "Give me my life," pleaded the sun after Maui, the demigod, had lassoed it. "I will give you your life," replied Maui, "if you promise to go more slowly across the sky so the women may dry their cloth." To this day, the sun seems to pass more slowly over Haleakala, the House of the Sun. Such legends are still repeated by locals when they speak of nature's cauldron of power and destruction that helped create their island.

Recent evidence, however, credits other forces. Scientists believe that a hot spot exists beneath the earth's crust in the Pacific area and, as a consequence of periodic eruptions of this hot spot, a chain of volcanoes, the Hawaiian Islands, has been created. Centuries of submarine volcanic eruptions piled up successive layers of lava. Finally, this undersea volcano burst through the ocean's churning surface, and eventually reached a height of 12,000 feet above the Pacific Ocean. Nature then began to work her wonders from above, as wind, rain and the sea eroded the new rock, and streams ripped away at its surface, creating valleys. Ultimately, in the Haleakala area, two major valleys grew until they met, forming a long depression. Subsequent volcanic activity then filled the depression, while vent eruptions created symmetrical cones.

The persistent trade winds, carrying over 300 inches of rain per year, had an equally dramatic effect on Haleakala crater. Because these winds blow consistently in one direction, the crater has eroded unequally, and the vegetation differs correspondingly. Erosion has created two gaps in the crater: the Kaupo Gap on the south side, and the steeper Koolau Gap on the north side. Although it is possible to hike down both gaps, the Koolau gap is not recommended because it is steep and treacherous in the lower elevations.

According to volcanologists, Haleakala crater does not qualify as a volcanic cauldera because erosion has caused it to shrink about 2000 feet to its present 10,023 feet. Nevertheless Haleakala is not extinct but only dormant, and it can be expected to erupt again some day.

Statistically, the "House of the Sun" is a large, dormant volcano, covering an area of 19 square miles. It is 7½ miles long, 2½ miles wide, and 21 miles in circumference. Some 30 miles of well-marked trails invite the hiker to enjoy the awesome yet delicate beauty, and the unmatched serenity and solitude of the crater.

Hiking into the crater is serious business because of the distance involved, the terrain, and the altitude. Experienced hikers can plan their own trip from the information contained herein. For others, I recommend the following hikes.

Full-Day Hikes

Halemauu Trail to Holua Cabin.

This is a vigorous, eight-miles-round-trip, 1400-foot-gain hike over a foot and horse trail to the floor of the crater. Food and water are a must on the trail, although water is available at Holua Cabin.

Sliding Sands Trail to Holua Cabin, exit by Halemauu Trail.

Take this hike if you plan an overnight stay at Holua Cabin, and then exit via the Halemauu Trail the following morning when it is cool. This is a difficult 12-mile, 1400-foot-gain hike that requires sound physical condition.

Sliding Sands Trail to Kapalaoa Cabin, exit by Halemauu Trail.

This hearty, 13.5-mile hike features an overnight visit at Kapalaoa Cabin. In the morning you can traverse the crater floor, visiting the Bubble Cave, the Bottomless Pit, Pele's Paint Pot and the Silversword Loop.

Sliding Sands Trail to Paliku Cabin to Kaupo Village.

Hikers in good condition can take this 17.5-mile hike from the highest point on Maui to sea level. It covers the sparsely vegetated crater and the lush foliage of the Kaupo Gap. An overnight visit at Paliku is particularly rewarding, since the rich flora there is in marked contrast to the rest of the crater.

If you are able to spend more than one night in the crater, I recommend staying at Paliku Cabin one night and Holua the second. This will certainly enable you to enjoy the crater at a leisurely pace.

TRAIL MILEAGE

Sliding Sands Trail and connecting trails
Summit at 9,745 feet to:

Holua Cabin	7.4
Kapalaoa Cabin	5.8
Bubble Cave	6.5
Paliku Cabin	9.8
Kaupo Village	17.5

Haleamauu Trail and connecting trails
Park road at 8,000 feet to:

Holua Cabin	3.9
Silversword Loop	4.8
Bottomless Pit	6.2
Kapalaoa Cabin	7.7
Paliku Cabin	10.2
Kaupo Village	17.9

Lauulu Trail
Paliku Cabin (6,400 feet) to:

Kalapawili Ridge (8,630 feet)	2.3

On the Trail: The following descriptions of trails and highlights encountered along the way correspond to the numbers on the Haleakala Crater map. There are six interconnected trails in the crater listed on the hiking chart.

1. Sliding Sands Trail.

The trail begins just above the visitor center on the south side of Pakaoao (lit., "sun comes through the portals of heaven") Hill at 9745 feet. Pause before descending for a broad panorama of the crater. With the map, a number of prominent points can be identified. Koolau (lit., "windward") Gap is to the north and Kaupo Gap is south of Paliku.

Pakaoao Hill has an interesting history as a place used by wayfarers and by robbers who waylaid them. The southwest slope is covered with stone-walled enclosures used by the Hawaiians as sleeping shelters and for protection from the elements.

As you begin your hike, you will agree that the Sliding Sands Trail is appropriately named. The cinders and ash that make up the area around the trail were expelled from vents during eruptions and were carried by the wind to line the inner crater. As you descend, the contrasts of the crater become evident. The lush forest of the Koolau Gap to the north and the usually cloud-enshrouded Kaupo Gap to the southeast stand in marked contrast to the seemingly barren terrain around you. After 2 miles and a 1700-foot descent, you reach a trail marker which identifies a spur trail that leads to Kaluu o Ka oo, a cinder cone. At the end of this short spur trail, you stand atop a cinder cone and can examine its design up close.

You will find some common crater plants in this area. The pukiawe (*Styphelia tameiameiae*) has tiny, evergreen-like leaves with reddish-white berries. The plant with yellowish flowers on upright stems is the Kupaoa (*Dubautia menziesii*) which, literally translated, means "fragrant." A few isolated silversword plants (see Haleakala Trail Description #13 below) are located just off the trail.

2. Puu O Pele ("Hill of Pele")

Although legend has it that Pele, the Hawaiian goddess of fire, lives in Kilauea Volcano on the island of Hawaii, this hill was named in her honor. With binoculars you are able to see Kapalaoa Cabin on the right. The building visible to the north is not Holua Cabin but a horse corral used by maintenance crews.

3. Trail Junction.

You have hiked 3.9 miles and are now on the crater floor at 7400 feet. By now you may have heard the feral goats bleating along the west walls of the crater. Indeed, you may be able to spot them clinging to the rugged slopes or feeding in the small, cool canyons. These goats are the descendants of those brought to the islands by Captain George Vancouver in the late 1700s. While they seem to delight and entertain visitors, they create a number of problems, since they eat the silversword, mamane and other desirable vegetation. The goats are particularly plentiful on the slopes, ridges and canyons above the cabins.

Flora in the area includes a native grass (*Trisetum glomeratum*) that grows in tufts or bunches and is known locally as mountain pili (lit., "cling, stick"). Mountain pilo (lit., "bad odor")(*Coprosma montana*) is common and may be identified by its orange berries and handsome bush. A favorite of foraging pigs is the bracken fern (*Pteridium aquilinum*), a fern found in many lands which may be familiar to you.

TRAIL MILEAGE
(From Junction #3)

East to:
Kapalaoa Cabin	1.9
Paliku Cabin	6.0
Kaupo Village	13.7

North and east to:
Bottomless Pit	1.7
Bubble Cave	2.7
Holua Cabin	3.5
Paliku Cabin	5.9
Kaupo Village	13.6

4. Bubble Cave

This natural shelter was created when a part of a bubble collapsed in the center, providing a convenient entrance. The bubble was blown by gases that held its shape until the surrounding lava cooled. Today, it offers a unique rest or lunch stop, and it has been used as an overnight camp many times.

5. Kapalaoa Cabin (7270 feet)

Kapalaoa (lit., "The whale or whaletooth") Cabin is one of three comfortable cabins maintained by the Park Service. Tent camping is not permitted in this area. Behind the cabin and about 1000 feet above on a ledge on a ridge are the remains of a heiau constructed by early Hawaiians for religious purposes. There are also a number of platforms and shelters along the ridge, but the climb is difficult and should be approached with caution. There are no markers or trails to lead the way. Views are superb, particularly of the south coast of Maui.

6. Aa Lava Flow

The hike to Paliku Cabin crosses a lava flow composed of aa (lit., "rough") lava, a Hawaiian term that is accepted today by geologists to identify lava whose surface cooled, hardened and fractured into rough pieces. The trail is difficult, with extremely rough underfooting.

Hawaiian "snow," the whitish lichen mentioned in Hiking Area #15, is very common on the aa lava. About midpoint, Paliku Cabin is visible straight ahead across the lava flow, nestled in a grove of native trees.

7. Oli Puu ("hill to appear") Junction

Get out the poncho, if you have not already, for the rainy portion of your crater experience usually begins at this point if you are going on to Paliku Cabin. A different type of lava (pahoehoe) appears in this area. It is a smooth variety that frequently forms lava tubes when the outside chills and hardens and then the still-molten interior flows out of the cool shell.

Very pretty mamane (*Sophora chrysophylli*) trees are conspicuous with their yellow blossoms, a favorite of feral goats. But the favorite of hikers is the ohelo (*Vaccinium reticulatum*) bush, which bears a tasty red, edible berry in late summer. It is rather prolific in this section of the crater.

Although the jet-black berries of the Kukaenene (lit., "goose dung") (*Coprosma ernodeoides*) bush are eaten by the nene, the Hawaiian goose, they are used as an emetic by Hawaiians. You are well-advised to avoid them.

TRAIL MILEAGE
(From Junction #7)

East to:	
Paliku Cabin	1.3
Kaupo Village	9.1
Northwest to:	
Bottomless Pit	2.7
Holua Cabin	5.0
Park Road via Halemauu Trail	8.9

8. Paliku Cabin (6400 feet)

Unless you have cabin reservations or a water-proof tent and sleeping bag, you won't spend too much time enjoying Paliku (lit., "vertical cliff"). The rain and wind blow for a while, stop, and then start again. It is precisely the yearly

300-plus inches of rain, however, that create a lush garden of native and introduced plants and make Paliku the most enchanting spot in the crater. The cabin is located at the base of a pali (lit., "cliff") that towers 1000 feet above. The campground is in a grassy area to the front-right of the cabin. When it is raining, some hikers use the covered shelter that serves as a stable.

Behind the cabin and surrounding the pit toilet, the akala (lit., "pink") (*Rubus hawaiiensis*), a Hawaiian raspberry, grows profusely. It bears a large, dark, edible berry that is rather bitter to eat but makes a delicious jam. In addition to the mamane described above, other native trees include the ohia (*Metrosideros collina*), the island's most common native tree, with its gray-green leaves and red flowers that look like those of the bottle-brush plant. The kolea (lit., "to boast") (*Myrsine lessertiana*) is conspicuous around Paliku, since it grows to a height of 50 feet and has thick leaves and dark purplish-red or black fruit. Hawaiians used the sap of the bark to produce a red dye for tapa cloth.

In addition to the goats and pigs that you might have the opportunity to observe, watch for the nene (*Branta sandvicensis*), the Hawaiian state bird. After disappearing, this native bird was reintroduced on Maui in 1962 and has since done fairly well. The Park Service has a program to raise goslings at the park headquarters and return them to the wilds in due course. The natural breeding cycle is difficult, owing in part to a number of introduced predators such as mongooses, pigs, and feral dogs and cats, for whom the eggs and the young goslings are easy prey.

The nene has adapted to its rugged habitat on the rough lava flows far from any standing or running water. The most noticeable anatomical change has been a reduction of webbing between the toes, creating a foot that better suits its terrestrial life.

If you are fortunate enough to spot a nene, don't be surprised if it walks up to you. They are very friendly birds and have been known to enjoy a petting!

9. Lauulu Trail and Kipahulu Valley

The trail begins behind Paliku Cabin and zigzags up the north wall 2.3 miles. Although the trail is not maintained, a "good" hiker can make it. Kipahulu (lit., "fetch from exhausted gardens") Valley lies beyond the pali and extends to the ocean and Oheo bridge. It is a genuine wilderness area that has been explored by a few daring souls who have hiked the difficult Lauulu (lit., "lush") Trail to Kalapawili (lit., "twisting") Ridge. From the ridge there are excellent views of the Hana coast, the Kaupo Gap and the crater. Hiking into Kipahulu Valley, however, is prohibited by the Park Service.

10. Kaupo Gap

Kaupo (lit., "landing at night") Trail follows Kaupo Gap and is a popular exit from the crater, but one that presents a transportation problem getting from Kaupo Village to central Maui, Lahaina or Hana. Although the road has been improved around the south side to Kaupo Village, it remains rugged and bumpy. Hitchhiking from Kaupo is only a remote possibility, since few cars are found on the road. However, if you are up to a nine-mile hike to the Oheo bridge, a ride from there to your destination is more likely.

The trail is well-defined and initially follows the base of the pali, from which a number of waterfalls and cascades are visible, as well as views of the coastline and the Kaupo area. You are using some muscles you didn't use in the crater, for your descent is 6000 feet in eight miles, which means you will be "braking" all the way. You may hear goats and pigs along the trail, although they may not be visible in the heavy brush.

About halfway down, the trail becomes a jeep road, used by the Kaupo Ranch, which may be used by four-wheel-drive vehicles with permission.

11. Aa Lava Flow

On the connection trail between the east and west sides, you are crossing the ancient divide between the Koolau and

Kaupo valleys, in addition to one of the most recent lava flows in the crater, which is 500-1000 years old. Feral goats are particularly active in this area, browsing on the lower branches and the bark of the mamane trees. Just before the trail junction, on your north side, is a prominent wall constructed of lava rock which was once used to corral cattle being driven into the crater to graze on the lush, rich grasses at Paliku.

At the junction, the vertical, slablike columns of rock protruding from the ridge are volcanic dikes that are remnants of the ancient divide between the valleys. Puu Nole (lit., "grumbling hill") opposite the dikes is a small cinder cone with a number of silversword plants on its slopes.

12. Bottomless Pit

In recent years a safety railing has been built around this pit, which is 10 feet in diameter and 65 feet deep. Some locals claim the pit extends to the sea. The pit was formed by superheated gases that blasted through from beneath.

In an earlier period, Hawaiians threw the umbilical cords of their newborn children into this pit—among others—to prevent (they believed) the children from becoming thieves or to ensure them strong bodies later in life. The Hawaiians' motive for this practice varied.

As you continue on the trail northwest about 100 yards beyond the pit, look for Pele's Paint Pot—a colorful area that was created by the many different minerals present in the magma. Many volcanic "bombs," hunks of lava in spherical shapes, are identifiable.

13. Silversword Loop

Don't fail to hike this short (0.4 mile) loop trail to view some of the best examples of silversword in the crater. Silversword (*Argyroxiphium sandwicense*) is probably the single most popular attraction in the crater. The plant is endemic to the islands and, thanks to protection by the Park Service, it is recovering and thriving. Its enemies are the feral goats, who eat the plant, and "feral" visitors, who pick the firm, silver-colored leaves for souvenirs.

A relative of the sunflower, the silversword has stiff, stiletto-shaped leaves and a brilliant flower stalk. Typically, the plant will grow from four to twenty years, its age marked by the size and number of silverswords at the base. Then in a brilliant burst, the flower stalk will grow from one to nine feet in height, sometime between May and October and will produce hundreds of purplish sunflowerlike blooms. After flowering only once, the entire plant dies and the seeds are left to reproduce. The crater species does surprisingly well, surviving on 16-50 inches of rain annually. Viewers familiar with the yucca blossom of the Southern California desert will find them a familiar sight, although the two plants are not related.

TRAIL MILEAGE
(From Holua)

Silversword Loop	.9
Pele's Paint Pot	2.2
Bottomless Pit	2.3
Bubble Cave	3.3
Kapalaoa Cabin	3.8
Paliku Cabin	6.3
Kaupo Village	14.1
Observation Point at summit	7.4
Haleamauu Trail to Park Road	3.9

14. Holua Cabin

A day or two's stay is particularly enjoyable at Holua (lit., "sled"). It is fun to watch the feral goats browsing in the canyons and on the cliffs behind the cabin and to explore the caves and lava tubes in the area.

Behind the cabin, about 25 feet up the cliff, is a cave that Hawaiians once used as a campsite. About 100 yards to the front-right of the cabin is a lava tube through which you may walk with the aid of a flashlight. It is about 150 feet long and is exited through a hole in the roof. There are grass beds used by recent hikers near the exit. A recent archeological survey found the remains of an adult male and two young children entombed in the part of the tube between the entrance and spatter vent—known as Na Piko Haua (lit., "the hiding

place of the navel cords"). Ancient Hawaiians hid the
umbilical cords of their newborn in such pits. It was regarded
as unlucky for the child if the cord was found.

At dusk, be certain to listen for the strange call of the
dark-rumped petrel (*Pterodroma phaeopygia*), which sounds
like the barking of a small dog. This white-and-black sea
bird makes its nest on the crater slopes, where it produces
one white egg annually. For six months afterward, it flies in
from the ocean each day to tend the nest, arriving after
sundown. Its "bark" seems to assist it in finding the nest
after nightfall.

15. Halemauu Trail

Halemauu (lit., "grass hut") Trail, constructed by the
Civilian Conservation Corps in the 1930s, remains in good
condition. Horse and mule pack trains enter and exit the
crater via Halemauu on a series of switchbacks for most of
the 3.9-mile course, ascending 1400 feet to the park road.

After a night's rest at Holua Cabin, the trail provides an
enjoyable hike with spectacular views of the crater and the
east side—when the weather is clear. There are a number of
comfortable spots at which to rest in the morning shade.

16. Hosmer Grove

The grove contains a small campground and picnic area
with six tables, fire grills and a tenting area. It is a delight for
an overnight visit. It's a good, convenient spot to camp if you
wish to see the sunset or the sunrise from the summit of
Haleakala.

A short, self-guiding trail is adjacent to the campground,
and trail pamphlets are available to assist in identifying the
native and introduced plants. Many of the introduced plants
were established by Dr. Ralph S. Hosmer, the first Territorial Forestor of Hawaii. There are excellent examples of
sugi (Japanese cedar), cypress, cedar, juniper, Douglas fir,
eucalyptus, spruce and a number of pines. Native plants
include sandalwood, mamane, aalii, mountain pilo, ohelo
and kupaoa.

N
W E
S

To Wailuku

Haleakala Observatory (9,745 ft.)

Science City

Skyline Tr. (8.0)

Haleakala National Park

Ballpark Junction

Polipoli Park

Kahua Tr.

Trail ·····
Jeep Rd. – – –
Trail Mileage ( )

17   Skyline Trail

Rating: Strenuous. Elevation loss 3800 feet.

Features: Views of Lanai, Kahoolawe and Hawaii, and West Maui Mountains, cinder cones, historical sites, Polipoli Park, and native and imported flora.

Permission: None.

Hiking Distance & Time: 8 miles, 4 hours (to Polipoli Park)

Driving Instructions:

From Lahaina (59 miles, 2 hours) southeast on Route 30, right on Route 380, right on Route 36, right on Route 37, left on Route 377, left on Route 378 to the summit (Park headquarters is 11 miles before the summit).

From Wailuku (40 miles, 1½ hours) east on Route 32, right on Route 36, then as above.

Introductory Notes: The Skyline Trail begins on the south side of Science City. As you approach the summit and Puu Ulaula (lit., "red hill") Observatory, a road on the left leads to Science City, where, a hundred yards farther, before

entering Science City, another road bears left, marked by a
sign indicating the park boundary. Follow this road to a sign
which identifies the Skyline Trail. At this point, you are at
the 9750-foot level on the southwest rift of Haleakala
Crater. As noted on the sign, the jeep road is ordinarily
closed to vehicles because the instruments used in astro-
nomical research at Science City are sensitive to dust.

On the Trail: On a clear day, the big island of Hawaii can be
viewed to the southeast. The island of Kahoolawe (lit., "the
carrying away by current"), seven miles off the coast, is
uninhabited and is used by the military for bombing practice.
Known locally as the Cursed Island, Kahoolawe was once
used as a base by opium smugglers. The ghost of a poisoned
smuggler is said to walk at night. Between Maui and
Kahoolawe, tiny, U-shaped Molokini (lit., "many ties")
appears. The pineapple-producing island of Lanai is to the
northwest.

On this trail, you will descend a total of 3800 feet. The
first 1000 feet is your "moon walk" over rugged and barren
terrain, with several cinder cones and craters along the rift.
You are compensated, however, by a spectacular panorama
of the island. The eye easily sweeps the offshore islands, the
West Maui Mountain range, central Maui and the east side.
The Maui "neck" is clearly visible from the trail.

The mamane (lit., "sex appeal") tree line begins at the
8600-foot level, and the native scrub becomes denser and
more varied. A mamane tree (*Sophora chrysophylla*) in full
bloom is a beautiful sight, with its bright yellow flowers. It is
a favorite of feral goats, who eat them greedily and quickly
exterminate them in an area. The gate across the jeep trail at
the 8200-foot level marks the halfway point to Polipoli. At
this point, you have hiked four miles.

An additional two miles brings you to the Papaanui-
Kahikinui Junction at 7000 feet. On the left of the trail is a
large open area that was used as a baseball field by members
of the Civilian Conservation Corps during the 1930s and
the area is called "Ballpark Junction" by locals. From the

junction it is a one-mile trek to a point where a sign identifies the Haleakala Ridge Trail. After 0.3 mile from the sign, take the Polipoli Trail to the camping area some 0.6 mile farther, passing through dense stands of cypress, cedar and pine on the way.

Polipoli Park has camping facilities, water, flush toilets —and a stand of redwood trees. There are also numerous easy family hiking trails in the vicinity. Between May and July delicious Methley plums are a favorite of locals, who swarm over the area with baskets and pick them. All along the trail, you can expect to be surprised by California quails with their curved head plumes, ring-necked pheasants, and chukars, which are brownish-black ground-dwelling partridges.

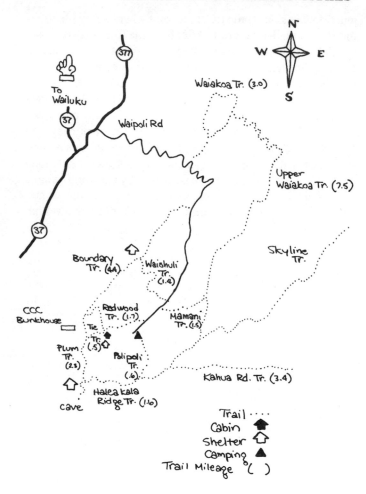

18 Polipoli Park

Rating: See individual hikes.

Features: Plums, redwoods, solitude, fresh and crisp air, birds, free camping.

Permission: Tenting or cabin permits from State parks Division. Trail shelters are first come, first served. No fee and no permits required.

Hiking Distance & Time: See individual hikes.

Driving Instructions:

From Lahaina (50 miles, 2 hours) southeast on Route 30, right on Route 380, right on 36, right on Route 37 past Kula, left on Route 377 for 0.4 mile, right on Waipoli Road to end (10.5 miles).

From Wailuku (31 miles, 1½ hours) east on Route 32, right on Route 36, then as above.

Introductory Notes: The Waipoli Road to Polipoli (lit., "mounds, bosom") is a winding, bumpy route. The first 3½ miles are paved, but the next 7 miles are difficult and not recommended for passenger cars. My Volkswagen bus has never had a problem, however.

Polipoli Park is an enjoyable hiking and camping area for the whole family. Although the road is difficult, it is well worth the effort for an overnight visit. On weekends, usually in the early morning hours, you may be treated to some local hang-gliding enthusiasts "doing their thing" on the slopes of Haleakala. These daring young men, harnessed to kites that measure about 12 to 20 feet, take off around the 6000-foot level for a five-minute glide to the Forest Reserve entrance below.

Polipoli Park is only a part of 12,000 acres that also comprise the Kula (lit., "open country") and Kahikinui (lit., "great Tahiti") Forest Reserve on the upper west and south slopes of Haleakala Crater. Native forests of koa, ohia and mamane have been largely destroyed since the 1800s by cattle, goats, fires and lumbering. During the 1920s a major reforestation and conservation project was begun by the state, and it was continued in the 1930s by the Civilian Conservation Corps. The result was the planting of hundreds of redwood, Monterey cypress, ash, sugi, cedar, and numerous types of pine.

Early mornings and evenings are usually clear, with fog, mist and light rain arriving later in the day. Annual rainfall is 20-40 inches, and the nights are generally cold—unexpected by visitors to Hawaii. Indeed, winter nights frequently have below-freezing temperatures. But don't be discouraged: at least those pesky mosquitoes are absent!

A number of birds may be found in the park along the trails. With the aid of a small booklet, *Hawaii's Birds,* published by the Hawaiian Audubon Society, I have been able to identify the ringnecked pheasant (*Phasianus colchicus torquatus*), the chukar (*Alectoris graeca*), the California quail (*Lophortyx californicus*) with its distinctive head plume, the skylark (*Alauda arvensis*), and the ever-present mynah (*Acridotheres tristis*), which is probably the noisiest bird known to man. Indeed, the mynah, one of the most common birds on the island, is both intelligent and entertaining. One clue to recognizing it is that it walks rather than hops.

Redwood Trail, 1.7 miles, 1 hour (trail rating: hardy family). Elevation loss 900 feet.

Aptly named, this trail is my favorite at Polipoli because of the hundreds of redwoods (*Sequoia sempervirens*) that were planted as part of the reforestation program in 1927. Since that time, these wondrous giants have grown to a height of about 90 feet, and some measure four feet or more in diameter at the base. The hike is a particular joy for those familiar with the California redwoods. To walk among these majestic trees, to delight in their fragrance, to feel the soft sod from accumulated needles underfoot, and to view the sun trying to force its way through their dense foliage is an overwhelming experience.

The trail begins a short distance from the campground off the west side of Waipoli Road at 6200 feet. A state park cabin is located a couple of hundred yards from the road alongside the trail. The view from the cabin is exciting and the sunsets can be very beautiful. Don't miss either. From the cabin, the trail follows a circuitous route through stands of redwoods and other conifers to the 5300-foot level. Markers identify many of the trees along the way, such as Mexican pine, tropical ash, Port Oxford cedar, sugi, and some junipers.

At trail's end, you are met by a generous garden of hydrangeas that seem to engulf the ranger's cabin, which is occupied only when the area is being serviced. However, flowers are not the main attraction here. Locals flock to this part of the park yearly to pick the Methley plum, which grows abundantly just below the cabin. The plums usually ripen in June, although they may be sweet by the end of May.

Tie Trail, .5 mile, ½ hour (trail rating: hardy family). Elevation loss 500 feet.

A trail shelter located at the junction of the Tie Trail and the Redwood Trail contains four bunks. The Tie Trail does what the name implies: it connects the Redwood Trail with the Plum Trail, descending 500 feet through stands of sugi, cedar and ash. The Tie Trail junction is .8 mile down the Redwood Trail. The Tie Trail joins the Plum Trail .6 mile from the ranger's cabin.

Plum Trail, 2.3 miles, 2 hours (trail rating: hardy family)

The trail begins at the ranger's cabin and the old Civilian Conservation Corps (CCC) bunkhouse at the west end of the Redwood Trail and runs south until it meets the Haleakala Ridge Trail. The trailhead is a favorite spot to pick Methley plums during June and July. Both the ranger's cabin and the old CCC bunkhouse may be used for overnight shelter, but both are rough and weathered and do not provide drinking water or other facilities. Often, during late afternoon, the trail becomes shrouded by fog or mist, which makes for wet, damp, cool hiking. You should be prepared with rain gear.

Although the plums attract hikers, there are stands of ash, redwood and sugi trees as well. The trail terminates on a bluff overlooking the Ulupalakua ranch area of Maui. An overnight shelter sleeping four is located here.

Polipoli Trail, .6 mile, ½ hour (trail rating: family)

This trail connects the camping area of the park with the Haleakala Ridge Trail. From the campground it passes through rather dense stands of Monterey pine, red alder, cedar, pine and cypress, all of which emit delicious fragrances. Many fallen and cut trees provide an abundant supply of firewood for campers.

Haleakala Ridge, 1.6 miles, 1 hour (trail rating: family). Elevation loss 600 feet.

For a full panorama of the island, the Ridge Trail provides the best views, since it is not as heavily forested as other parts of the park. It begins at the end of the Skyline Trail, at 6550 feet, and follows the southwest rift of Haleakala to join the Plum Trail at 5950 feet. The Haleakala Ridge Trail can be reached from the south end of the Polipoli Trail, 0.6 miles from the campground.

Monterey pine, cypress, eucalyptus, blackwood, hybrid cypress and native grasses are identified by markers along the trail. At trail's end, be certain to investigate a small ten-by-twenty-foot dry cave located in a cinder cone and used as a trail shelter. An eight-by-ten-foot ledge in the cave provides a relatively comfortable king-sized bed. A spur trail to the cave is clearly marked and easy to follow.

Boundary Trail, 4.4 miles, 4 hours (trail rating: hardy family)

The Kula Forest Reserve boundary cattle guard on the Polipoli Road marks the trailhead for the Boundary Trail. This trail descends gradually along switchbacks to follow the northern boundary of the reserve to the ranger's cabin at the Redwood-Plum Trail Junction.

The trail crosses many gulches that abound in native scrub, ferns and grasses as well as stands of eucalyptus, Chinese fir, sugi, cedar and Monterey pine. About ½ mile below the cabin, fuchsia bushes proliferate to the point of obscuring the trail. As you pass through this garland of delicate, red, lanternlike flowers, a clearing encircled by eucalyptus trees appears across the fence. Hikers wishing to connect with the Kula road must jump the fence and cut across the pasture to Kula Sanitarium about 4 miles below. Numerous points along the trail provide views of central Maui.

Waiohuli Trail, 1.4 miles, 1½ hour (trail rating: hardy family). Elevation loss 800 feet.

The rough, poorly maintained Waiohuli (lit., "churning water") Trail begins on the Polipoli Road at 6400 feet and goes straight down the mountainside to meet the Boundary Trail at the 5600-foot level. Indeed, rather than looking for the trail, simply follow the ridge line. The trail passes rough, low native scrub, young pine plantings and grasslands, and then wanders through older stands of cedar, redwood and ash.

Don't be apprehensive. There is no chance of getting lost as long as you follow a straight line. You will eventually join the Boundary Trail, which is well-maintained and clearly identifiable. At this junction, another overnight shelter is conveniently located.

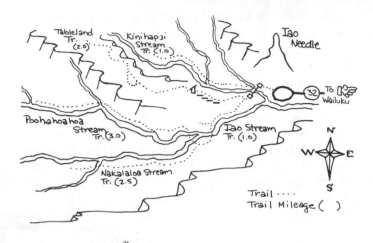

19 Iao Valley

Rating: See individual hikes.

Features: Strawberry and common guavas, swimming, native flora, and views of central Maui, Iao Valley and Iao Needle.

Permission: None.

Hiking Distance & Time: See individual hikes.

Driving Instructions:

From Lahaina (24 miles, 1 hour) southeast on Route 30 to Wailuku, left on Route 32 to end.

From Wailuku (3 miles, ¼ hour) west on Route 32 to end.

Introductory Notes: Few people dispute that Iao (lit., "valley of dawning inspiration") Valley is one of the most beautiful valleys on Maui. It has long been a favorite of locals and tourists, who come to see the Iao Needle, the John Kennedy Profile, and the splendid tropical gardens and streams.

The area surrounding the state park is owned by the Maui Land and Pineapple Company; however, trails and paths have been "established" by locals and visitors and are used without securing permission. Use extreme caution when hiking off the trail in the streams, for the mossy rocks are treacherous. I have lost count of the twisted ankles and bruised knees I have received there, not to mention the times I have fallen into the stream. On all but the tableland hike, you can expect to get wet, since the trail frequently crosses the stream.

The whole family can enjoy Iao. There are casual family walks as well as more difficult hikes to challenge the adventurer. However, do not hike the streams when it is raining in the higher areas, because of the possibility of flash flooding. Each year the streams are altered considerably by the seasonal rains and resulting floods; therefore, pools, small waterfalls and other such features mentioned here may no longer exist. You can expect, however, that other pools and waterfalls will have been created.

Tableland Trail, 2 miles, 1½ hours (trail rating: hardy family). Elevation gain 500 feet.

From the parking lot at the end of the road, cross the bridge and follow the paved walk to the lookout shelter. A good trail to the tableland begins behind the shelter over a railing. The first ½ mile is relatively steep, with a gain of 300 feet. At this point, the Needle is all but indistinguishable as you view its west side across Kinihapai Stream. As you continue, watch for a short, steep trail on the left that leads to the top of the ridge. Follow this spur trail and continue along the razorback for spectacular view of Iao Valley and Wailuku. The razorback detour then rejoins the Tableland Trail, which is not steep for the rest of the hike. Between August and October, strawberry guavas flourish along the trail. This red, walnut-sized fruit may be eaten whole or after removing the small seeds inside. Sample them, but for the most succulent selections do your picking on the tableland.

In addition to the profuse gauvas, ti plants and ferns abound in this area. As you approach the tableland, the strawberry guavas become more abundant. The tableland is identified by the tall, waist-high grass on a large, flat area

ringed by guava trees. Pick, eat and enjoy the varieties of
guavas. The common guava may be eaten whole, although
some prefer to eat only the inner portion, which is sweeter
without the skin.

A tasty drink may be concocted from the guavas you
bring back from your hikes if you have a blender. Wash the
whole guavas and fill the blender. Add one cup of water.
Reduce to a syrup, and strain. Mix this syrup with your
favorite base (orange, grapefruit, passion fruit) to taste.
Serve with ice or after chilling.

When you return to the parking lot, be sure to walk to the
stream below for a swim. There are a number of sizable
pools. You'll probably share the pools with local children
who frequent the area; better yet, find your own private pool.

Iao Stream, 1 mile, ½ hour (trail rating: family).

After crossing the bridge at the parking lot, take the path
to the left, which descends to Iao Stream. A well-defined
trail then extends for ½ mile along the stream. From then on,
it is necessary to make your way by walking in the stream or
over the rocks or along the bank. Numerous pools along the
way, varying in depth and width, are fine swimming holes.
Guavas are very common in Iao, so be particular and eat
only the sweetest ones. Strawberry guavas are farther up the
stream, but are not as abundant there as on the tableland.

At the one-mile point, the stream divides, with Nakalaloa
Stream to the left and Poohahoahoa Stream to the right. The
relative seclusion and the inviting pools make this area a
favorite of skinny-dippers and nude sun bathers. If you blush
easily, you had better wear blinders.

**Poohahoahoa Stream, 3 miles, 2 hours (trail rating:
strenuous).**

Beyond the Poohahoahoa Stream junction with Iao
Stream and Nakalaloa Stream it is unlikely that you will find
other people. Use extreme caution, since Poohahoahoa (lit.,
"heads getting together") Stream on the right narrows in
places, making it necessary to swim the stream or to crawl
over rocks in order to progress. Indeed, there are places

where ropes are needed to negotiate narrow canyons. This is a very rugged area where flash flooding is common. The canyons are extremely beautiful in this remote wilderness.

I do not recommend that any but the most experienced hikers take this trail. the terrain is rugged and the rocks treacherous. Bear in mind that even the largest rock or boulder may roll or shift if enough weight is applied to it. If you continue, don't get careless. Make your way carefully and cautiously and always take the easiest path.

Nakalaloa Stream, 2.5 miles, 2 hours, (trail rating: strenuous).

Nakalaloa (lit., "complete forgiveness of sin") Stream on the left from the junction is not as narrow or as difficult to hike as is Poohahoahoa. Until 1984 it was possible to see the small, fern-lined grotto pictured on the cover of *Hiking Maui*. Since then storms and flooding have destroyed this dreamlike place.

More delights await the hiker upstream. There are not only a number of large pools in which to swim, but also a natural slide that drops the slider into a large pool. Only the most experienced hikers should continue beyond this point, for the terrain is rugged and the pitfalls many. Remember, most stream rocks are worn smooth and may be wet and mossy, making them treacherous. Don't be careless.

Beyond the slide, it is possible to follow an old trail and pass through the mountains to Olowalu on the southwest side of the island. This route was used by the ancient Hawaiians. A stream on the left continues along the base of the pali through a narrow canyon. It is necessary to climb along the nearly vertical walls at some points. Do not attempt to hike alone here, or without rock climbing equipment.

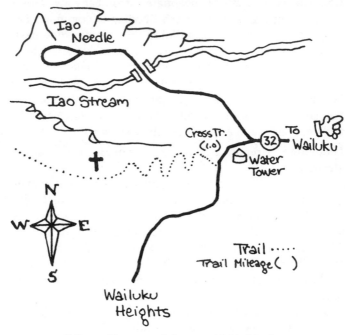

20   Cross Above Wailuku

Rating: Hardy family. Elevation gain 1000 feet.

Features: Views of Iao Valley and central Maui.

Permission: None.

Hiking Distance & Time: 1 mile, 1 hour.

Driving Instructions:

> *From Lahaina* (23 miles, 1 hour) southeast on Route 30 to Wailuku, left on Route 32, bear left at junction to Wailuku Heights. Look for telephone pole No. 5 on right. Park in turnout on left.

> *From Wailuku* (2 miles, ½ hour) west on Route 32, then as above.

Introductory Notes: In 1956 students from St. Anthony High School in Wailuku placed a cross above the town. Since then, they have replaced the original cross with one that can withstand the elements. Each year the seniors at the school, as part of an annual graduation project, hike to the cross for general repairs and maintenance work.

On the Trail: The trailhead is to the right of telephone pole No. 5. This is an enjoyable hike for the whole family, even though the first ¾ mile is almost straight up. The views into Iao Valley from a number of places along the trail are breathtaking. There are numerous overlooks before reaching the cross that offer views and a chance to catch your breath.

If you have any energy remaining when you reach the cross, it is worth the extra effort to continue up Kapilau (lit., "sprinkle of rain on leaves") Ridge for spectacular views into Iao Valley. On a clear day, waterfalls and cascades are visible in the recess of Iao. Use extreme caution, for the spine of the ridge narrows to a few feet at points, with steep vertical cliffs on each side.

It is easy to become preoccupied with Iao Valley, but there are also unobstructed views of central Maui and a generous panorama of the island.

Trail ····
Jeep Rd. ---
Trail Mileage ( )

21 Waihee Ridge

Rating: Strenuous. Elevation gain 1500 feet.

Features: Views of Waihee Canyon and Valley, central Maui, the north side; fresh-water spring.

Permission: None.

Hiking Distance & Time: 2.7 miles, 3 hours.

Driving Instructions:

From Lahaina (32 miles, 1¼ hour) southeast on Route 30 to Wailuku, right on Route 32, left on Route 340 (Kahului Beach Road) through Waihee, left on road to Camp Maluhia to trailhead on left 0.8 mile from Route 340.

From Wailuku (11 miles, ½ hour) east on Route 32, left on Route 340, then as above.

Introductory Notes: The Waihee (lit., "slippery water") Ridge trail and area are under the management of the Hawaii State Department of Land and Natural Resources and are regularly maintained.

On the Trail: From the parking area, pass through a turnstile and cross the pasture, following red "R/W" markers. You may be surprised by grazing cattle in the heavy brush along the road. Relatively sweet common and strawberry guava abound along the trail. Shortly, a gate across the road marks the border of forest-reserve land. If the gate is locked, passage is provided 20 feet to the right of the gate. In a few hundred feet the road ends and a foot trail begins. It turns right and climbs a ridge through an area of grass, ferns and trees.

The trail is marked every ¼ mile. There are a number of overlooks into Waihee Canyon and to the north into Makamakaole (lit., "not without intimate friends") Gulch. At the ¾-mile point and beyond for a distance, there are superb views of the valley. Thereafter, the trail switchbacks to the 1½-mile point and to a flat, grassy tableland that is wet and boggy but usually passable. One of the rewards of the trip is the fresh spring water on the edge of the tableland.

Be on the lookout for edible thimbleberries (*Rubus rosaefolius*), which grow profusely in this area. These red berries grow on a small bush with white flowers.

From the spring it is one mile to Lanilili (lit., "small heaven") Peak and breathtaking views of the north side of the island and of the surrounding valleys.

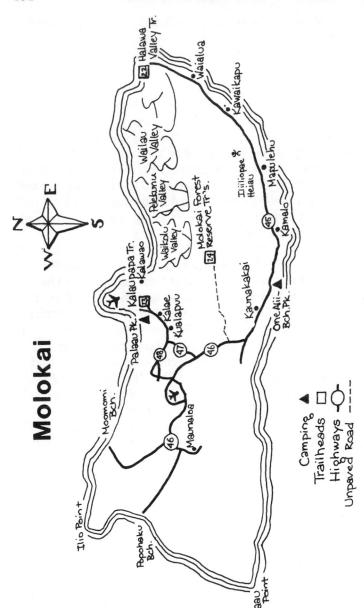

Molokai

N W E S

Camping
Trailheads
Highways
Unpaved Road

Molokai

The Island

Molokai is the island for a person who feels that Hawaii is overdeveloped and over commercialized and is looking for good outdoor experiences. The fifth largest island in the Hawaiian chain—37 miles long and 10 miles wide—Molokai was once known as the "Lonely Island" because the native sufferers of Hansen's disease (leprosy) were once banished here by the monarchy. Today, perhaps in response to an effort to change the island's image and to reflect more accurately its character, Molokai is known as the "Friendly Island." Locals still wave to passing motorists, shout greetings across the street to friends, and congregate in the few bars and restaurants in Kaunakakai, Molokai's town, to "talk stories" with friends and visitors. The slow-paced, relaxed life style is infectious.

Politically, Molokai is part of Maui County, and like the "Valley Isle" Molokai was created by two volcanoes. Mauna Loa is a shield volcano on the west side rising to 1381 feet, and Kamakou on the west side is the island's highest point at 4970 feet. It is along the range of mountains and valleys on the east and north sides of the island that the best hiking trails are to be found. Indeed, the four valleys on the north coast, Waikolu, Pelekunu, Wailau and Halawa, offer outstanding outdoor experiences. Practically speaking, only Halawa is accessible on foot. The others can be reached by helicopter or, in summer during calmer seas, by boat.

Although Molokai has retained a "nontourist," "low-key" style, it still offers adequate accommodations. There are a couple of hotels and a couple of condominiums offering satisfactory-to-first-class rooms and apartments, a number of car-rental agencies offering a wide range of vehicles, and a few good restaurants. A problem for the visitor is the lack of public transportation. Presently, hitchhiking in Maui County is illegal (check the law for any change) but a person may stand on the roadside. Most drivers understand, and I haven't had any problems getting rides on Molokai.

Camping

Palaau State Park, located nearly in the center of the island at 1000 feet elevation and eight miles from Kaunakakai, is the best of the three camping places on Molokai. A pavilion, restrooms, picnic tables, grills and water are available, at the usual state park fee—free! (I camped there for a week over the July 4, 1981, holiday and did not share the campground with one other person). It is a very comfortable, cool campsite, a short walk from the Kalaupapa trailhead.

The one beach camping area on Molokai is at One Alii County Beach, a few miles east of Kaunakakai. It has the same amenities as Palaau State Park, but a fee ($1 in 1981) is charged. Reservations may be made through the County of Maui (see Appendix). There is no swimming beach here or nearby. Indeed, the only good swimming beaches on Molokai are on the west side near the Sheraton Molokai Hotel and at a few places on the east side.

Wilderness camping is allowed in the Molokai Forest Reserve without a fee, by permission of the Division of Forestry (tel. 553-5019). At Waikolu Lookout in the reserve there is a pavilion, water, restrooms, and barbecue pits. It is located 13.4 miles from Kaunakakai, and 10 miles of this distance is on a rough forest road which is passable in a conventional vehicle only during the dry part of the year.

Hiking

Molokai offers some particularly interesting hiking and backpacking experiences. With the exception of Halawa Valley, the trails included are infrequently traveled. Kaulapapa does entertain many visitors daily, but few hike the trail—most fly to the peninsula or ride in on mules.

Oahu—Hanauma Bay

Maui—Waimoku Falls

Breadfruit

Kauai—Kalalau Beach and Valley

Maui—Iao Needle

Coconuts

Nene, Hawaii's state bird

Hawaii—Devastation Trail

Maui—along the Hana road

Maui— Hana road

Heliconia

The Wailau Valley on the north shore and the Wailau "trail" require special note. Wailau Valley is one of the few nearly pristine places in Hawaii that are accessible on foot—almost. The trail up the valley to the pali (cliffs) and the trail from the road on the south side of the island (trailhead is at the road leading to the Iliiliopae Heiau, 15 miles east of Kaunakakai) to the pali topside are well-defined and in satisfactory condition, but the 3000-foot descent of the pali is very difficult. On it, the trail is where the hiker can manage. The Wailau Trail should not be attempted by anyone who is not experienced in Hawaiian terrain or does not possess considerable outdoor skills. I suggest that you join a hiking group, such as a group of the Sierra Club, which usually makes an annual trek into Wailau, or else hire the services of a local person who will guide you. There are a number of persons on the island, particularly in Halawa Valley, who will serve as guides. Ask around. There are also a number of local boatmen who take people in and out of Wailau in the summer when the ocean allows safe passage. (In 1981, the fee was $30 per person one-way.) In any event, Wailau is an exciting experience. There are a number of camping spots along the beach and others on a 50-foot rise above the beach on the east side of the valley. The valley abounds with bananas, plums, mountain apples, guava, thimbleberries, and fresh-water prawns and shellfish. Locals who spend the summer in the valley are usually very generous with advice and with their catches.

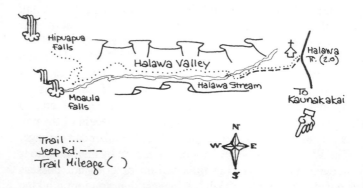

Trail ....
Jeep Rd. ---
Trail Mileage ( )

22   Halawa Valley

Rating: Hardy Family.

Features: Waterfalls, swimming, fruits.

Permission: None.

Hiking Distance & Time: 2 miles one-way, 1 hour.

Driving Instructions:

(28 miles, 1½ hours) From Kaunakakai drive east on Route 45/450 (posted both ways) to Halawa Valley. When the road levels in the valley locate a small church and a dirt road on the left. A sign directs hikers to Moaula Falls to park in a turnout across the road from the church.

Introductory Notes: Halawa (lit., "curve") Valley would most certainly be on anyone's list of the best places to visit in Hawaii. It contains all that a person expects in Hawaii—a good, pleasant hiking trail, fruits, and a generous pool in which to swim at the base of Moaula (lit., "red chicken") Falls. The valley is about ½ mile wide at the beachfront and about three miles deep. It was once heavily populated, but a tsunami in 1946 and almost annual flooding have discouraged permanent residents.

On the Trail: From the parking area on the main road, follow the dirt road past the church and a number of houses on both sides of the road. Do not turn right or left off the road, but follow it for ½ mile to its end. A foot trail continues past a couple of houses and alongside a stone wall on the left for about 150 yards. Then make a right turn (marked in 1981) directly to the stream. Scout around for the easiest and safest place to cross Halawa Stream. The trail continues on the opposite bank of the stream in the shade of giant mango (*Mangifera indica*) trees, whose fruit when ripe—usually March to October—is absolutely delicious. The large, pear-shaped fruit with orange pulp is quite sweet and juicy. The wood from these large, beautiful trees has been used for craftswood, furniture and gun stocks. From the stream, the trail passes under the mango trees and up a short rise to where it intersects a trail paralleling the stream. The fork to the right goes to the beach over private land. The fork to the left, our trail to the falls, passes countless more mango trees and noni (*Morinda citrifolia*), or indian mulberry, from whose roots and bark a yellow and a yellowish-red dye were produced. The small, warty-looking fruit was eaten in times of famine. It is a small evergreen with large, shiny, dark-green leaves. From here to the next stream crossing, the trail parallels a water pipe. It also passes by and bisects the remains of numerous taro terraces which once yielded great quantities of taro, from which the Hawaiian staple, poi, is produced. After you cross the north fork of Halawa Stream, Moaula Falls is about one hundred yards distant. Before you swim at Moaula, you should know about the legend of the moo (lizard) who lives here. It is safe to swim only if moo is happy, which can be determined by placing a ti leaf in the pool. If it floats, all is well; but if its sinks, well, you're on your own!

About 75 yards from the north fork stream crossing and just before the falls, a spur trail bears off to the right and up the cliff for about 150 yards to where it divides. One fork goes left up a steep bank and leads to the pool at the base of upper Moaula Falls. The other fork goes right and is soon lost in the brush. If you continue through the brush, Hipuapua (lit., "tail flowing") Falls is about one-fourth mile distant. Be extremely cautious on both side trails. The trail to upper

Moaula Falls is mostly on a nearly vertical wall where a wire has been placed to aid the climber. It is not for the faint-hearted.

The trail to Hipuapua is not clear, and a rockslide before reaching the falls makes passage difficult. However, 500-foot Hipuapua Falls is worth the effort, although the pool at the base is not as large as Moaula's. Look for mountain apples (*Eugenia malaccensis*) on your way to Hipuapua. These lemon-sized apples, when ripe, are deep-crimson with a pure white pulp and a large round seed. They make an ideal snack after a swim at Moaula.

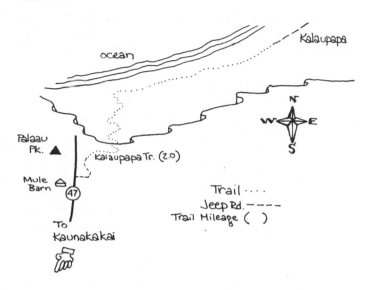

23 Kalaupapa

Rating: Strenuous. Elevation loss 1600 feet.

Features: Historical sites, views.

Permission: None to hike, but arrangements must be made to be met at trail's end by one of the two tour companies. No one is allowed to travel unescorted on the peninsula. Persons under 12 years may not visit Kalaupapa. If you ride the mules, a peninsula tour is part of the cost. If you wish to make your own arrangements, contact one of the following: Ike's Scenic Tours, 567-6437, or Damien Tours, 567-6171. Advance reservations are not necessary, but I suggest you call for the peninsula tour as soon as you arrive on Molokai.

Hiking Distance & Time: 2 miles one-way, 1½ hours.

Driving Instructions:

(9.6 miles, ½ hour) From Kaunakakai drive west on Route 46/460 (posted both ways), right on Route 47/470 (posted both ways) to the entrance of Palaau State

Park just beyond the Molokai mule barn. Go right on a
dirt road at the Park's entrance and drive to the trailhead.

Introductory Notes:

> "To see the infinite pity of this place,
> The mangled limb, the devastated face,
> The innocent sufferers smiling at the rod,
> A fool were tempted to deny his God.
>
> He sees, and shrinks; but if he look again,
> Lo, beauty springing from the breast of pain!
> He marks the sisters on the painful shores,
> And even a fool is silent and adores."

After a week on the Kalaupapa peninsula in 1889, where
he spent much of the time playing with leper children,
Robert Louis Stevenson left this bit of verse with the sisters
when he departed. I do not believe that anyone can visit
Kalaupapa without being affected, some profoundly. Certainly these 4½ square miles, which are bounded by vertical
2000-foot cliffs on the one hand and a rough sea on the
other, have changed a great deal since that first day that
Father Damien de Veuster set foot on shore in 1873. This
first white resident of the peninsula was dedicated to aiding
the forsaken souls who were banished to this leper colony.
Many were tossed overboard from the ships that brought
them and did not survive the swim to the shore. Those who
did survive found an inhospitable society where children,
women and the seriously ill were exploited by other sufferers
from leprosy and where survival of the fittest was clearly the
rule. For 16 years, until leprosy took his life, Father Damien
attended to the spiritual, medical, and material needs of the
populace. He built a church, but he also built houses, a
hospital, and, perhaps most importantly, a patient society
where exploitation was replaced by cooperation. After
Father Damien's death in 1889, Brother Joseph Dutton and
many others carried on his work. Today, Hansen's disease is
controlled with the use of sulfone drugs, so that it is not
necessary to isolate sufferers. The peninsula is now under
the authority of the National Park Service, and Kalaupapa is
likely to become a national park soon. Meanwhile, the 100-

plus patients who remain are guaranteed a home as long as they choose, but they are free to leave. Years ago, the Catholic Church began considering the question of sainthood for Father Damien. Robert Louis Stevenson expressed the feeling that the patients had for Damien during his life, and many have had after discovering this remarkable man. In 1890 Stevenson concluded a letter to Rev. C. M. Hyde, who had been severely critical of Damien, by writing, "Well, the man who tried to do what Damien did, is my father, and the father of the man in the Apia bar, and the father of all who love goodness; and he was your father too, if God had given you grace to see it."

On the Trail: Before descending the trail, walk to the guard rail by the U.S. Navy facility for a fine view of Kalaupapa (lit., "the flat plain") below. The peninsula was built long after the rest of Molokai by Kauhako (lit., "the dragged large intestines"), a 405-foot shield volcano. It is best to begin your hike before 8:30 a.m., when it is cooler and you won't be troubled by the mules. The trail is wide and safe in spite of its abrupt descent and 26 hairpin turns. But some places have deep holes from the mules so caution should be exercised to avoid a twisted ankle. Throughout the day, shade trees and trade winds offer relief from the heat. There are numerous places along the trail to view Kalaupapa. This is not the trail used by Father Damien; it was farther east. According to "Ike," a patient who conducts peninsula tours, the so-called Damien trail was dynamited after the priest's death by the people who owned a ranch in the flat country above the cliffs. It seems that some of the patients would ascend the trail and steal and slaughter cattle for food. After the trail reaches the beach, it is about ¼ mile to the mule corral and a paved road which leads to Kalaupapa town. Your tour guide will meet you at the corral. You are not allowed to wander beyond this point. It is permissible to stroll along Puwahi (lit., "broken conch") Beach, where you are likely to encounter patients pole-fishing or throwing nets. The patients are very friendly and are quick to talk stories.

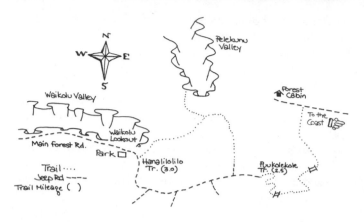

24   Molokai Forest Reserve

Rating: See individual hikes.

Features: Mountain and coastal views, native flora.

Permission: Camping permits from Department of Land & Natural Resources.

Hiking Distance & Time: See individual hikes.

Driving Instructions:

(13.4 miles, 1 hour) From Kaunakakai drive west on Route 46/460 (posted both ways) for 3.4 miles to a dirt road on the right just before a large white bridge and opposite the "Moloka Aggregate Co." Go right on the dirt road for 10 miles to Waikolu Lookout. Do not attempt this road in a conventional car unless the road is dry. The road is not posted, so stay left whenever you meet another road. However, do not turn left into the pineapple fields. You will be ascending a ridge and heading in the direction of tall trees. If you do not reach the forest reserve (posted) after driving 5.7 miles on the dirt road or a forest Boy Scout camp after 5.9 miles, you are on the wrong road. From the camp, it is 3.2 miles to the "sandalwood boat" and from there 1.0 to the lookout. Unless you are driving a jeep or four-wheeled-vehicle, DO NOT drive farther. Even when dry, the road beyond is deeply rutted.

Introductory Notes: The "sandalwood boat," or Lua Na Moku Iliahi (lit., "pit of the sandalwood ship"), which is alongside the road one mile from the lookout, deserves a note. It is believed that a chief had this pit constructed to the dimensions of the hold of a sailing ship. Sandalwood trees were then cut and the logs were placed in the pit and sold by the pitful, which was also a shipful.

Waikolu (lit., "three waters") Lookout provides a dramatic view into narrow and steep Waikolu Valley from a 3700-foot perch. During wet periods countless waterfalls burst forth from the cliffs. A recently constructed water tunnel provides most of the water for the south side of the island. On a clear day, the view is breathtaking. However, on a cloudy day you may see your shadow on the clouds—the rare Spectre of the Brocken.

Hanalilolilo Trail, 3 miles one-way, 2 hours (trail rating: strenuous). Elevation gain 500 feet.

Hanalilolilo (lit., "disappearing place") gets its name from the illusion that some experience here. They say that as they approach Hanalilolilo (the area above Waikolu Valley) it seems always to be receding.

From Waikolu Lookout walk 0.2 mile (Waikolu Valley should be on your left) on the road to the trailhead, posted on the left side of the road. The entire hike is through a native forest of ohia lehua and a variety of fern. Initially the trail climbs in the forest at the head of Waikolu Valley. Views of the valley are not good here because the ohia trees are so profuse. The ohia is a noble tree, a native tree and the most common tree in Hawaii. It has gray-green leaves and tassel-like red flowers that look like those of the bottle-brush plant. Legend holds that the flower is a favorite of Madame Pele, the goddess of volcanoes, and if it is picked without the proper incantation she will cause rain to fall. There are many varieties of ferns along the trail. The most common tree fern in the island is the Hawaiian tree fern, Hapu (*Cibotium menziesii*), whose trunks have been used to make tikis, fences, pathways and orchid logs. In times of famine, the fleshy stems of the fern were eaten. The ulei (*Osteomeles anthyllidifolia*), or Hawaiian rose, is particularly abundant near the trailhead. It is a single, sweet-scented thornless rose and usually found on a low shrub and sometimes growing to a height of 14 feet. Its hard wood, known for its pliability, has been used for bows, back scratchers, and javelins used in the Hawaiian game of pahee.

A short distance from the trailhead, you pass a water-works on the left side, from which you may get your last view of Waikolu Valley. About ½ mile beyond, be alert for a large lava-walled, fern-lined pit on the right. It is the type of formation that when combined with lush tropical foliation is one of the treasures of Hawaii. From this point to the tableland, the trail twists and turns through a heavily foliated native rain forest where the safest footing is on the roots of the trees. One false step and it's mud to the knee. Avoid the soft, damp mudholes in the middle of the trail.

The tableland is two miles from the trailhead. The trail emerges from the ohia forest onto a large, football-field-sized, grassy area which is very wet and boggy. Make your way to the highest place (bear to the left), which is near the center of the tableland. When you reach the high point, look for a trail (taped in 1981) on the left. This ¼-mile trail descends through a rain forest and ends at a precipitous point overlooking Pelekuna (lit., smelly from lack of sunshine) Valley.

After returning to the tableland, retrace your steps to the trailhead, or go in the opposite direction and bear to the right into the ohia forest on a ½-mile trail (marked in 1981) that will take you to a spur road off the main forest road. Continue a short distance on the spur road to where it joins the main road. To the left the main forest road goes to the Puu Kolekole Trailhead and to the right it returns to the Hanalilolilo Trailhead and the Waikolu Lookout some two miles distant. The main road to Waikolu Lookout twists, turns, and drops through two gulches. Bear to the right at all intersections.

Puu Kolekole Trail, 2½ miles one-way, 2 hours (Trail rating: strenuous). Elevation gain 800 feet.

Of the two trails in the forest reserve, Hanlilolilo is better and more interesting. It is well-defined and it offers an outstanding view of Pelekunu Valley. If you decide to try Puu Kolekole, you should hike it after Hanalilolilo since you are close to the trailhead.

The Puu Kolekole (lit., "scarred hill") Trailhead is reached by walking 2.5 miles from the Waikolu Lookout. Stay on the main forest road by bearing left at all road junctions. Only a jeep or 4WD vehicle can traverse this part of the road. After two miles, a road to the left extends about 50 yards and becomes the Hanalilolilo foot trail. Stay on the main road for another ½ mile to its end at a small, flat turnaround.

At road's end, bear to the left where the trail descends into a deep, fern-lined gulch. This part of the trail is fairly well-defined, although there are places where ferns and thimbleberries block the trail and scratch the legs unless you have long pants. You should tape or mark your route, for the trail makes numerous turns before reaching a concrete bridge across a gulch. From here, the trail ascends the opposite wall of the gulch to an area of low brush, where a view of Kaunakakai is possible. From this vista the trail makes a sharp left, ascends a short distance and then descends into another gulch, where the trail is covered with brush. However, it is now only a short distance to a 50-yard-long tunnel on the left through the mountain. A second concrete bridge is just beyond the tunnel. After you cross the bridge a well-defined trail to the left goes about 200 yards and ends at an abandoned waterworks. Thimbleberries are particularly sweet and abundant here, growing on a small bush with white flowers. The main trail continues up the side of the gulch and soon levels in a tangle of guava (*Psidium gaujava*) trees, whose lemon-sized fruit is high in vitamin C. Walk due north after ascending the gulch. There are bits of trail here and there, but do not wander far unless you pick up a distinct trail about 100 yards from the gulch. From here it is a short distance to the Puu Kolekole road near some tall cypress trees. Go left on the Puu Kolekole road for 400 yards to reach the forestry shack and trail's end, or go right on that road a short distance to a number of vistas of the south side of Molokai. From the first viewpoint the Puu Kolekole road goes 4.5 miles south to reach Route 45/450 about 2 miles east of One Alii Beach Park and 4 miles east of Kaunakakai. Hike the Puu Kolekole road from the first viewpoint if you do not have to return to Waikolu.

Oahu

The Island

Take a walk along Waikiki Beach any time of the day, any time of the year, and you will understand why this, the third largest of the Hawaiian Islands, is called "the gathering place." Everyone is here—Japanese, Chinese, Filipinos, Blacks, Samoans, Germans, Canadians, Australians and others.

What is it that brings people here from all over the world? Can it be the air temperature, which seldom varies by more than 10 degrees, with a year-round average of 75° F? Can it be the 80° water temperature at Waikiki Beach? Can it be the enchantment of precipitous cliffs and heavily overgrown valleys existing as backdrops to a city covered with asphalt and high-rise buildings? Can it be the fascinating blend of the multi-ethnic population? Can it be the life style in which individuality reigns supreme, and muumuus and cutoffs, oxfords and bare feet, tuxedoes and swimsuits intermingle in the restaurants and discotheques? Can it be the surf, the music, the sun-tanned bodies, the aloha spirit, the wild fruits, the hiking, the camping, the slow pace of life, the . . . .?

The truth is that Waikiki, and Honolulu, are all of these things. The truth is that long before the first-time visitor arrives, Hawaii has transmitted its message via the plaudits of happy visitors, the media, and the Hawaii Visitors Bureau. The truth is that the first-time visitor has been primed for pleasure long before his jumbo 747 flies over Diamond Head and lands in Honolulu. For most people, there are no disappointments, and they return again and again.

Indeed, the crowds are sometimes so great that people spill off the sidewalk onto Kalakaua Avenue in order to get by casual strollers. Combine the 3 million-plus tourists who visit Oahu annually with the 762,565 permanent residents

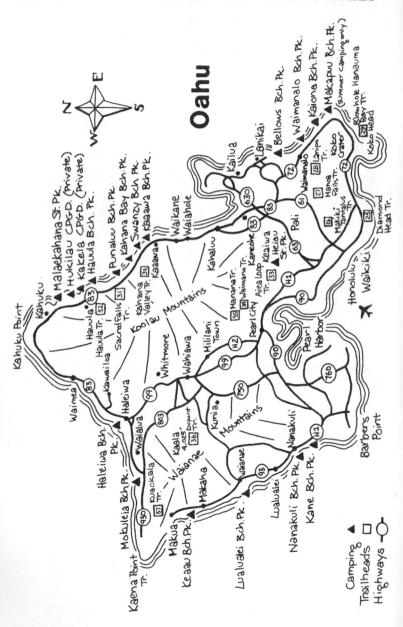

(over 80% of the state's population) and you have a lot of people on a rather small island.

Honolulu was not an original Hawaiian city. It was established by the followers of Captain Cook who, in search of anchorage, discovered this protected deep-water bay. Honolulu (lit., "protected bay") grew rapidly and was soon recognized as the trading and business center of the islands by King Kamehameha III. The official capital of the Kingdom of Hawaii was moved from Lahaina, Maui, to Honolulu in 1850. For the next 85 years, the southeast end of the city remained a swamp where taro was cultivated and ducks and other marsh birds roamed freely. However, in the past 45 years Waikiki has been dramatically altered from its humble beginnings to become one of the most recognized beaches in the world.

The two mountain ranges of Oahu and indeed the whole island were created by volcanic eruptions. Oahu took shape as lava flows filled the area between the ranges until the present 607 square miles existed. In time, the Koolau mountain range on the east side and the Waianae mountain range on the west side were further sculpted by natural forces, so that both have both gently sloping parts and steep, precipitous parts.

Camping

Hiking can be an exciting way to see Oahu, and camping can make your visit an inexpensive one. Since camping is a popular activity with local people, make your plans in advance and obtain permits as soon as you arrive on the island. There are two state and two private campgrounds on the island and 15 county beach parks where camping is permitted. Camping is free at the state and county parks. The private campgrounds charge (1981) $.50 per person over 12 years old.

Camping is permitted at only two campgrounds in the state park system on Oahu. The campground at Keaiwa Heiau State Park is in a shaded, wooded area near the trailhead of the Aiea Loop Trail. Malaekahana State Park is just north of Laie on the east coast, on a beautiful white, sandy beach. It is a new park and campground, with new facilities. Reservations are required, and camping permits are granted for a maximum of one week. Reservations for these two parks may be made by mail, but the applications must be received by the Department of State Parks at least seven calendar days in advance of the date the permit is to be in effect. (All addresses are in the appendix.)

The City of Honolulu operates 63 recreational areas located on all parts of the island. Camping is permitted at 15 places, all of which are beach parks. Permits are not issued earlier than two weeks before the day of occupancy. Camping is allowed from Fridays through Wednesdays; there is no camping on Thursdays. Permits can be obtained from the Department of Parks and Recreation in Honolulu or at any of 10 satellite city halls located around the island. (All addresses are in the appendix.) All the campgrounds have cold-water showers, drinking water and restrooms. Most of the beach parks receive heavy use, so they are not always clean and the facilities are not always in good operating order. The campgrounds at Waimanalo, Swanzy, Kahana Bay, Punaluu, Mokuleia, Keaau, Lualualei, Nanakuli and Kahe are recommended, since they are usually clean and they have ample space for camping. Trailer camping is permitted at all of the parks where tents are allowed except Lualualei Beach Park and at Kaaawa Beach Park. Trailers must be self-contained, since there are no electrical or sewer connections.

Zions Securities (address in Appendix) in Laie operates two private beach campgrounds. Both campgrounds— Kakela and Hukilau—are satisfactory if the state or county parks are not available. Permits can be obtained at their office in Laie. A fee is charged.

The camper should keep in mind that most of the campsites on Oahu are in heavily populated areas or in areas accessible to population centers. Consequently, all of the ills—thievery, damage to equipment, drunkenness—of urban living are present. Campers should not leave valuables and equipment unattended or unprotected.

Hiking

There is more to Oahu than world-famous Waikiki, Diamond Head and Pearl Harbor. On the windward (east) side of the island are the Hawaiian communities of Hauula and Laie, where numerous valley hikes and beach camping, away from the crowds, await the outdoorsperson. The north shore of Oahu may well be the surfing capital of the world, with the Banzai Pipeline, Sunset Beach and Waimea Bay.

Although there are no hikes on Oahu to compare to the Kalalau Trail on Kauai, the trails in Haleakala Crater on Maui or the Mauna Loa Trail to the 13,677-foot summit on Hawaii, there are trails to excite and to challenge the hiker. The Dupont Trail to Mt. Kaala, the highest point (4025 feet) on Oahu, is an outstanding hike, and the hikes to Sacred Falls and into Makiki Valley are equal to any of the valley hikes on the other islands.

While most of the hikes on Oahu are short-distance, part-day hikes, I have included a wide selection of trips from short, easy family walks to long, difficult hikes. I have not included areas from which hikers are forbidden by law (protected watershed) or where the terrain is dangerous and unsafe even though local people may boast of their adventures into these places. Each year numerous injuries and some fatilities occur where people have hiked in spite of the prohibition. For example, a prominent sign at the end of the Manoa Falls Trail warns hikers not to climb above the falls, where the terrain is brittle and treacherous. Nevertheless, numerous injuries, rescues, and even deaths have been recorded there in recent years. However, good judgment and a regard for the time-tested rules of hiking are good protection.

In the following descriptions, driving distance and time start at Waikiki. The fine public transportation system on Oahu deserves a special note. Many visitors make the mistake of renting a car when "The Bus"—yes, that's what it's called—is convenient, reliable, comfortable and inexpensive. The Bus makes regular stops at most places of interest on the island. Unquestionably, The Bus is the best bargain on Oahu. For 50¢ you can ride nearly 100 miles around the island: From Honolulu, The Bus travels along the east coast, passes across the north shore and returns through the central part of Oahu to Honolulu. The system is so reliable that I have included instructions for taking The Bus to the trailheads.

The one shortcoming of the system is that backpacks are not allowed unless they can be carried on the lap or stored under the seat. Call 531-1611 from 5:30 a.m. to 10 p.m. daily for information and schedules.

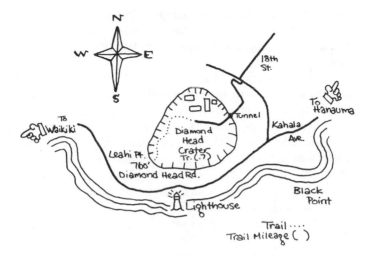

Trail · · · ·
Trail Mileage ( )

25   Diamond Head

Rating: Family. Elevation gain 550 feet.

Features: Panorama of greater Honolulu area, historical site, extinct volcanic crater.

Permission: None.

Hiking Distance & Time: 0.7 mile one-way, 1 hour.

Driving Instructions:

From Honolulu (4 miles, ¼ hour) drive south on Kalakaua Ave., right on Diamond Head Road and around to east side of crater, left at sign marked "Civ-Alert USPFO" opposite 18th St. Follow road through tunnel into crater to parking area on left.

Bus Instructions:

From Waikiki on Kalakaua Ave. take bus #57 ("Hawaii Kai/Sea Life Park") to 18th St. and Diamond Head Road at a sign marked "Civ-Alert USPFO." Follow this road into the crater.

Introductory Notes: Although the hike to the summit of Diamond Head is hot and dry, the panorama offered from the top and along the rim trail is striking. This is a "must"

hike for the whole family. Although a large part of the crater
and the surrounding area are on a military reservation, the
hiking trail is under the jurisdiction of the Division of State
Parks.

Without question, Diamond Head is the most photographed and the most readily identifiable place in Hawaii.
Before the arrival of Western man, the area was known as
Leahi (lit., "casting point"). In the early 1800's British
sailors found calcite crystals in the rocks on the slopes of the
crater and thought they were diamonds. Following the
discovery, the tuff crater was called Kaimana-Hila (lit.,
"Diamond Hill"), and today the world-famous place is
known as Diamond Head. Geologists estimate that the
crater was formed some 100,000 years ago by violent steam
explosions. During World War II Diamond Head was an
important bastion for the protection of the island. Gun
emplacements, lookout towers, and tunnels were concealed
in and on the walls of the crater. Although abandoned in
recent years, these places are interesting to investigate,
particularly for children. It is helpful to carry a flashlight,
since the trail passes through two short tunnels and up a spiral
stairway.

On the Trail: The trailhead on the northwest side of the
parking area is marked, and the trail is easy to follow to the
summit. Kiawe (*Prosopis pallida*) trees abound on the floor
of the crater. These valuable trees with fernlike leaves and
thorny branches are the descendants of a single seed planted
by Father Bachelot, a priest, in 1828 in his churchyard in
Honolulu. The tree is a source not only of fuel and lumber
but also of honey (produced from the flower), medicine,
tannin and fodder, which is produced from its beanlike
yellow pods containing 25% grape sugar.

As you continue along the gently rising trail to the first
concrete landing and lookout, you should be able to identify
a number of birds. Two species of doves, the barred dove
(*Geopelia striata*) and the spotted dove (*Streptopelia
chinensis*), are common and abundant on Ohau. The spotted
dove, the larger of the two, has a band of black around the

sides and back of the neck, which is spotted with white. The barred dove is pale brown above, gray below, and barred with black. You should also see the beautiful, bright red, male cardinal (*Richmondena cardinalis*) with its orange beak and black face.

The concrete landing is the first of many lookout points along the trail. You have a good view of the crater and are able to distinguish some of the bunkers and gun emplacements on the slopes and on the crest of the crater. Follow the steps and the pipe railing to the first tunnel. You cannot see daylight at the end of the tunnel, because it turns to the left at midpoint. A flashlight is not necessary to pass through the tunnel safely but is a comfort to small children, since it is dark. As you leave the tunnel, investigate the rooms in the concrete building opposite the exit, which were used for supplies and contained a power unit. Look for the bunker behind the building and hike to the left to a viewpoint overlooking the crater. A steep staircase—99 steps—leads the hiker into a short tunnel at the end of which is an observation room and the first view of Waikiki and the greater Honolulu area. Look for the room containing a spiral stairway. Climb the stairway and then the ladder that takes you to the top and to the summit of Diamond Head. The concrete building at the summit is situated on top of Leahi Point at an elevation of 760 feet. Keep a watchful eye on children, for the summit's flanks are precipitous. The observation point at the summit provides a shady and comfortable picnic spot as well as a panoramic view.

It is possible to hike completely around the rim of the crater and to return to the parking lot by cutting through the brush, but the trail is steep and dangerous due to loose volcanic rock and ash. Only confident hikers should attempt this alternative route to the parking area. You will find numerous observation points and gun emplacments around the rim similar to those at the summit.

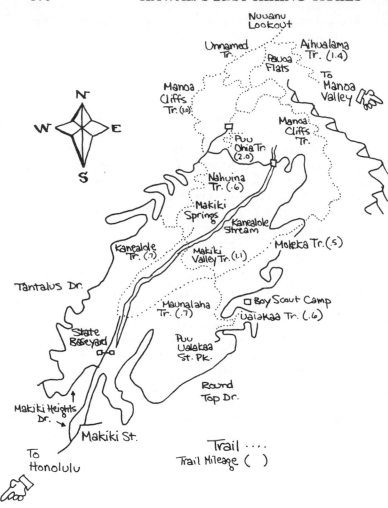

26 Makiki/Tantalus

Rating: See individual hikes.

Features: Mountain apples, Job's tears, native and introduced flora, valley views.

Permission: None.

Hiking Distance & Time: See individual hikes.

Driving Instructions:

To Makiki Valley From Honolulu (3 miles, ¼ hour) drive up Makiki St., turn left on Makiki Heights Dr. and continue straight on paved drive in Forestry "baseyard" (2135 Makiki Heights Dr.). Drive past a sign "Makiki Forest Recreation Area" to a parking area on the right just before a chain gate.

To Tantalus From Honolulu (6 miles, ¼ hour) drive up Makiki Street, turn left on Makiki Heights Dr., then go right on Tantalus. Drive three miles to the top, where there are a telephone-service road on the left and a trailhead marker.

Bus Instructions:

To Makiki Valley From Waikiki on Kuhio Ave. take bus #2 ("Liliha-Puunui" or "School-Middle St." to Beretania/Alapai St. Secure a transfer and walk toward the sea to Hotel St. Take bus #15 ("Pacific Heights") to Mott-Smith Dr. and walk toward the mountains to Makiki Heights Dr. and to the trailhead.

To Tantalus No bus service on Tantalus Drive or Round Top Drive.

Introductory Notes: There are three trails in Makiki Valley, two trails in the Tantalus area, two trails that connect the Tantalus area with Makiki Valley, one trail that joins Makiki Valley with Puu Ualakaa State Park, and one trail that connects Tantalus with Manoa Valley (see map). Consequently, there are trails to suit most hiker's interests and abilities. Your choices should be easy after consulting the maps and the trail narratives.

Tantalus and Round Top drives combine to make a popular auto tour above Honolulu. The many turnouts, which provide panoramas of Honolulu, are favorites of visitors and locals in the daytime and lovers in the evening. The two hikes that lead into the mountains from the top of the road are a delight for the whole family. Local students named this area "Tantalus" after the mythical Greek king. Tantalus

Mountain (2013 feet) was so named, it is suggested, because as the students hiked, the peak seemed to recede. (You may recall that Tantalus was punished by being made to stand in a pool of water that receded each time he tried to drink.)

You have a choice of numerous trailheads for the hikes included in this area. I suggest that you begin your hiking either at the Manoa Cliffs trailhead on Tantalus Drive or at the Puu Ohia trailhead, where Tantalus Drive becomes Round Top Drive (0.5 mile from the Manoa Cliffs trailhead on Tantalus Drive.) The Manoa Cliffs trailhead on Round Top Drive is on the mountain side of the road at telephone pole #55 opposite a turnout and parking area. Two other good choices of trailheads are the Aihualama trailhead near the base of Manoa Falls in Manoa Valley and the Makiki Valley trailhead.

Kanealole Trail, 0.7 mile one-way, ½ hour (trail rating: family). Elevation gain 500 feet.

The trail on the west side of Kanealole Stream is usually wet and muddy, but it is a gentler ascent than the Maunalaha Trail on the east side. The trail follows an old road that was once used by work crews to control the growth in the valley. Although the hike is uphill, there is abundant shade along the trail, which makes for a fairly cool and enjoyable hike for the whole family. Look on the left side of the trail as you ascend for surinam cherries (*Eugenia uniflora*) which, when bright red, are quite sweet. This small, ovate cherry from Brazil is a local favorite for making jelly. At the junction with the Makiki Valley Trail, you can follow it across the valley to the right or go left a short distance and connect with the Nahuina Trail, which will take you to Tantalus.

Nahuina Trail, 0.6 mile one-way, ½ hour (trail rating: hardy family). Elevation loss 600 feet.

Nahuina was constructed by the Sierra Club's Hawaii Chapter, which organized volunteers in 1979 to link the Tantalus and Makiki Valley hiking areas (see map). The idea was good because there is a lot of hiking pleasure to be gained from the loop hikes now possible. From the Manoa

Cliffs trailhead on Tantalus Drive, the Nahuina Trail is easy
to find. It is about 150 yards down the road on the left side
(east), at the end of a white guard rail. From the junction
with the Makiki Valley Trail, the Nahuina Trail heads north
to Tantalus Road.

Regardless of your point of departure, the first part of the
trail is in good condition. After a short distance, fallen trees
cross the trail and chest-high vegetation completely covers
it. (I suggest the Mokeka Trail on the northeast side of the
valley as a connecting trail between Tantalus-Round Top
and Makiki Valley.) If you take the Nahuina Trail, I urge
caution because it is usually muddy and slippery. On the
descent from Tantalus Drive, the trail is well-defined for a
short distance until a fallen, giant koa tree blocks the trail.
You can scramble uphill through or around the tangle of roots
and pick up the trail on the other side. From here almost to
the Makiki Valley Trail, be alert and cautious because the
trail is overgrown and difficult to follow.

Makiki Valley Trail, 1.1 miles one-way, 1 hour (trail rating: family)

This east-west trail traverses Makiki Valley. (The valley
was named after a type of stone found here that was used as a
weight for an octopus lure.) The trailhead on the west side is
about 2 miles up Tantalus Drive from Makiki Heights Drive,
north of a eucalyptus grove where the road makes a sharp
turn. The trailhead on the east side is about at the midpoint
of the Ualakaa Trail.

From the Tantalus Drive trailhead, the trail descends
eastward through a forest into Makiki Valley, passing the
Nahuina Trail on the left (north) and, shortly, the Kanealole
Trail on the right (south). At this second junction, pause to
look for springs in the brush to the left of the junction. The
grass and brush should be matted where other hikers have
made their way to the springs, 30 feet north of the junction.
It is an enchanting place to pause to enjoy the beauty and the
solitude. It is also a place to pick Job's tears (*Coix lacryma-jobi*), which are abundant. The black, blue-gray and white,

pea-sized beans of this plant are favorites with the local people, who string them into attractive necklaces, leis and rosaries. Ranging from one foot to six feet high, the plant is a coarse, branched grass with long, pointed leaves. The beans are easy for children to string with a needle and heavy thread.

From the junction, the trail turns in and out of small gulches and crosses a couple of small streams, passing through a richly foliated, forested valley. One of the many delights along this trail is the mountain apple (*Eugenia malaccensis*), which is abundant and within easy reach. What a treat! The apples are found on both sides of a stream in a very peaceful setting in which to pause and enjoy this succulent and red fruit. Up the hill from the stream at an unmarked junction, the Mokeka Trail goes to the left to meet the Manoa Cliffs Trail at Round Top Drive, the Makiki Valley Trail goes straight about ¼ mile more to end where it meets the Ualakaa Trail, and the Maunalaha Trail to the right goes to Makiki Valley and the baseyard.

Maunalaha Trail, 0.7 miles one-way, ½ hour (trail rating: family). Elevation loss 555 feet.

From the junction with the Makiki Valley Trail, the hike on the Maunalaha Trail is an easy downhill walk. The trail contours along Makiki Ridge, passing through avocado, juniper, eucalyptus and bamboo in the lower portion. Periodically, a break in the forest provides a good view of Honolulu and of Manoa Valley to the east. One of the most interesting trees in the valley is the octopus, or umbrella, tree (*Brassaia actinophylla*), whose peculiar blossoms look like the long, spreading arms of an octopus. The new blossoms are first greenish-yellow, then light pink and finally deep red. As the trail levels, it crosses a footbridge over a stream, passes through the territorial nursery, and returns to the baseyard parking area.

Moleka Trail. 0.5 mile, ½ hour one-way (trail rating: hardy family)

Joining the Makiki Valley and Tantalus-Round Top, the

Moleka Trail, like the Nahuina, was constructed in 1979 by volunteers organized under the leadership of the Sierra Club's Hawaii Chapter. Of the two trails, the Mokeka is in good condition and is easy to locate and to follow. The trailhead is on Round Top Drive opposite the Manoa Cliffs trailhead, southeast of the turnout and parking area.

Descending from Round Top Drive, you step into a natural garden of ti, ginger (both white and yellow), bamboo and the delightfully beautiful heliconia (*Heliconia humilis*), or "lobster claw," so named because the bright red bracts are similar to boiled lobster claws. The trail gently contours along the valley slope, providing numerous views into Makiki Valley. Be on the lookout for edible red thimble-berries along the trial, growing on a small, thorny bush with white flowers. About midway, a side trail to the left (east) will take you to Round Top Drive. Continue down and to the right to reach a junction with the Makiki Valley Trail. From the junction, the Makiki Valley Trail goes to the left to join the Ualakaa Trail and to the right across Makiki Valley. The trail ahead, the Maunalaha Trail, descends to the Makiki Valley baseyard.

Ualakaa Trail, 0.6 mile one-way, ½ hour (trail rating: family)

The newest trail on Oahu, Ualakaa (lit., "rolling sweet potato"), was constructed in 1980 by volunteers organized by the Sierra Club's Hawaii Chapter. The purpose was to connect Puu Ualakaa State Park with the Makiki/Tantalus hiking area.

The trailhead is 0.1 mile from the entrance of Ualakaa State Park at telephone pole #9 on the right side just as the road makes a sharp turn. From here, the trail ascends, paralleling Round Top Drive for a short distance until it meets, entering from the left, the Makiki Valley Trail. The Ualakaa Trail ends shortly on Round Top Drive just opposite Camp Ehrhorn, a Boy Scout camp.

Manoa Cliffs, 3 miles one-way, 2 hours (trail rating: hardy family). Elevation gain 500 feet.

Just 3 miles up Tantalus Drive, a sign identifying the trail and a spur road that leads to a Hawaiian Telephone Co. facility mark the trailhead for the Manoa (lit., "vast") Cliffs Trail. The trail is well-maintained and easy to follow. You are likely to share the trail with students from the University of Hawaii, since the area is used as an outdoor classroom. The initial, forested portion (1.2 miles) contours the hillside. A number of native and introduced plants, some of which are identified by markers, are found along the trail. According to the Division of Forestry, 33 native species of flora have been identified. You should not have any trouble finding two introduced plants whose fruit is edible. Guava (*Psidium guajava*) trees are particularly abundant throughout the area. The yellow, lemon-sized fruit is a tasty treat high in Vitamin C.

About 1 mile from the trailhead, you reach a junction. The trail to the left (north) is well-defined and will eventually join the Puu Ohia Trail at Pauoa Flats. You may choose to continue on this unnamed trail and to return to the Manoa Cliffs Trail via the Puu Ohia Trail. At the junction with the unnamed trail, the Manoa Cliffs Trail makes a sharp right and follows switchbacks up a hill for 0.2 mile to the Manoa Cliffs/Puu Ohia trails junction (actually, a pair of junctions 30 feet apart). Puu Ohia leads north (left) down the hill and south (right) up the hill while the cliffs trail continues east.

The remaining part of the Manoa Cliffs Trail hike contours the hillside above Manoa Valley. Spectacular views of the valley are possible from a number of viewpoints. Keep a sharp eye on small children, however, for parts of the hillside along the trail are steep. There are a number of overgrown trails leading off both sides of the trail which should be avoided. One spur trail, a short distance east from the Manoa Cliffs/Puu Ohia junction, switchbacks up the hill to meet the Puu Ohia Trail. The Manoa Cliffs Trail turns south and emerges on Round Top Drive at the other trailhead for this hike. Now it is 1.4 miles west (right) to your car via the road or 0.9 mile west to the Puu Ohia trailhead.

Puu Ohia Trail, 2 miles one-way, 1½ hours (trail rating: hardy family). Elevation gain 500 feet.

The Puu Ohia (lit., "ohia tree hill") trailhead is easy to find. It is 0.5 miles from the Manoa Cliffs Trailhead near the uppermost point of Round Top and Tantalus drives, where you will find a large parking area opposite the trailhead (the nearest street number is 4050). The first 0.5 mile of the trail follows a circuitous route up a hill. The trail then straightens and goes along the side of the ridge a short distance to where a number of trails lead off down to the right. Bear left and follow the trail to where it meets a paved road, then follow the road to its end at a Hawaiian Telephone Co. facility. The trail continues north from behind and to the left of the telephone building and descends to join the Manoa Cliffs Trail. As you descend, bear to the left to avoid the somewhat overgrown trails to the right and the one clear spur trail also on the right. This latter trail eventually meets the Manoa Cliffs Trail farther east. Soon you reach the Cliffs Trail, jog right 10 yards on it, and then continue north. The Puu Ohia Trail is wide but steep, so proceed with caution until you reach Pauoa Flats. Although the trail over the flats is level, it is usually wet and slippery and it has exposed roots which are potential ankle-busters.

Eucalyptus (*Eucalyptus robusta*) and paper-bark (*Melaleuca leucadendra*) trees dominate the flats area. The eucalyptus has thick, pointed leaves with a capsule type of fruit, while the distinguishing feature of the paper-bark tree is bark that can be peeled in sheets. This tree has been planted on the islands for conservation purposes in wet, boggy areas. There are a number of secondary trails on the flats where hikers have cut through the bamboo to vistas overlooking Manoa Valley to the east (right). Continue north (straight ahead) on the main trail to a lookout for a fantastic view of Nuuanu Valley, the Pali Highway, and Reservoir No. 4 in the Honolulu Watershed Forest Reserve. DO NOT hike beyond the lookout into the watershed area, which is protected by both law and good judgment.

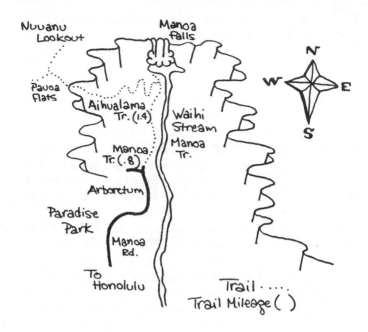

27 Manoa Falls

Rating: Family. Elevation gain 800 feet.

Features: Waterfall, swimming, fruits.

Permission: None.

Hiking Distance & Time: 0.8 mile one-way, 1 hour.

Driving Instructions:

From Honolulu (3 miles, ¼ hour) drive north on Manoa Road past Paradise Park and Lyon Arboretum to the end of the road.

Bus Instructions:

From Waikiki or Ala Manoa Center take bus #5 (Manoa-Waikiki) to Paradise Park at the end of the line. Walk up the road to the trailhead.

Introductory Notes: The trail to Manoa (lit., "vast") Falls is easily accessible from downtown Honolulu, which probably accounts for its popularity. You can expect to share the trail and the pool with local people as well as visitors. Nevertheless, pack a lunch and make the trip to the falls, for it is worth the time. To reduce the risk of a break-in, park your car in the lot at Paradise Park and walk the short distance to the end of the road.

In 1978, under the leadership of the Sierra Club's Hawaii Chapter, volunteers constructed the Aihualama Trail, which connects Manoa Valley with the Makiki/Tantalus hiking area, thus creating numerous hiking opportunities for a person who is looking for longer and more challenging hikes than the one to Manoa Falls. One suggestion for a delightful day's outing is to hike to Manoa Falls, follow the Aihualama Trail to Pauoa Flats, walk the Puu Ohia Trail to the Manoa Cliffs Trail, hike the Moleka Trail and finish your trip in Makiki Valley or at Puu Ualakaa State Park.

On the Trail: A chain gate and a foot bridge at the end of the road mark the trailhead for the hike into Manoa Valley along Waihi (lit., "trickling water") Stream. Most of the trail is muddy and a bit slippery because heavy rains have washed away soil around trees and exposed their roots. The heavy rains also sustain a heavily foliated area where vegetation common to damp areas is abundant. The trail is easy to follow through the forest reserve. There are some fruit trees along the trail, but the likelihood of finding fruit is slim because of the popularity of the hike. The yellow, lemon-sized guava may be found as well as the popular mountain apple. This succulent apple is small and red, has a thin, waxy skin, and is usually ripe in June.

At midpoint, the canyon narrows and the footing becomes wetter. There are a number of larger pools where you may see hikers swimming or catching prawns, crayfish or frogs. The latter are particularly plentiful. You should be able to see the falls from a number of points along the trail. The junglelike setting at the falls makes for an enchanting place to swim and picnic if it is not too crowded.

The Division of Forestry prohibits entry into the closed watershed beyond the falls. Violators might damage a protected area, and they face the prospect of court appearances and fines. Furthermore, numerous injuries and a few fatalities have been recorded as a result of people hiking in this prohibited area.

Aihualama Trail, 1.4 miles one-way, 1½ hours, 400-foot gain (trail rating: hardy family)

Do not mistake the precipitous and dangerous trail to the left of Manoa Falls for the Aihualama Trail. Beginning 50 feet from the falls, the Aihualama Trail follows a gentle zigzag path to Pauoa Flats. Enjoy the views provided along the first part of the trail. After 150 yards, turn for a good view of upper and lower Manoa Falls and across Manoa Valley to Waahila Ridge on the east side. A bit farther on, a view of the tip of Diamond Head and Waikiki is possible. The trail can be wet and muddy due to frequent showers throughout the year, but the rewards are great. Huge koa (*Acacia koa*) trees, with their crescent-shaped leaves, and interesting banyan (*Ficus benghalensis*) trees, with their aerial roots growing earthward from horizontal branches, combine with aromatic and delightfully beautiful ginger to excite the hiker.

After following the contour of the hill, the trail begins to switchback. Just before reaching Pauoa Flats, the trail cuts through a bamboo forest, which offers some interesting sights and sounds as the wind passes over the flatland and through the bamboo. At an unmarked junction, the Aihualama trail meets the Pauoa Flats trail. About 0.5 mile north, at the end of that trail, there are views of Nuuanu Valley. The trail to the left goes to the Puu Ohia/Manoa Cliffs trail junction.

28 Lanipo

Rating: Strenuous. Elevation gain 1600 feet.

Features: View from Koolau Mountain Range, native and introduced flora.

Permission: None.

Hiking Distance & Time: 3 miles one-way, 3 hours.

Driving Instructions:

From Honolulu (6 miles, ½ hour) drive southward on H-1 to Koko Head turnoff. Go left over freeway toward mountains, then right on Waialae Ave., and then take the first left, Wilhelmina Rise, to the top of the hill and Maunalani Circle, where a public-access passageway between fences marks the trailhead.

Bus Instructions:

> From Waikiki at Kalakaua/Kapahulu Ave. take bus #14 ("Maunalani Heights") to Sierra Drive/Lurline Drive. Walk up Sierra Drive to Maunalani Circle and the trailhead.

Introductory Notes: The Lanipo and Wiliwilinui (Hiking Area No. 10 in *Hiking Oahu*) trails are parallel hikes to peaks along the Koolau Mountain Range. Indeed, an experienced and daring hiker could join the two trails by hiking ½ mile along an extremely precipitous and dangerous ridge on the Koolau Range. Do not attempt this connecting hike alone. In any event, both hikes, while strenuous, are worth the effort, for the summit views of the east side of the island are stunning. Of the two, I prefer Lanipo because it is a 3-mile foot trail whereas the first 2½ miles of Wiliwilinui are on a jeep road. The Lanipo trail also skirts Kaau Crater.

On the Trail: The trail initially ascends along a fenced walkway for about 100 yards, to a point on Mauumae (lit., "wilted grass") Ridge. After a short descent, the trail traverses past a number of saddles along the ridge. The first two saddles are a bit steep, with loose rock underfoot, so that caution is advised to avoid sore feet or a twisted ankle. Since the flora along the ridge is mostly low scrub and low trees, views of the surrounding area are unobstructed. To the west (left) Palolo (lit., "clay") Valley extends north to Kaau (lit., "forty") Crater, which lies at the base of the Koolau Range ridge. The ¼-mile-wide crater, legend holds, was formed by the demigod Maui who, wanting to join Kauai and Oahu, threw out a great hook hoping to catch the foundation of Kauai. He gave a tremendous tug and loosened a rock. The rock fell at his feet where he was standing at Kaena Point on Oahu, while his hook sailed over his head and landed in Palolo Valley, creating Kaau Crater.

After the midpoint of the hike, the ridge narrows considerably. Thereafter, the trail is wet, muddy and steep, and it is necessary to grasp branches and roots of plants to continue. However, there are level places to rest and to enjoy a panorama of Diamond Head and the Honolulu area.

A variety of native plants can be identified. Look for ulei (*Osteomeles anthyllidifolia*), a single sweet-scented thornless Hawaiian rose; kawau (*Byronia sandwicensis*) a Hawaiian holly tree with white blossoms and black berries; and the common yet beautiful and interesting ohia lehua (*Metrosideros collina*), a plant that varies in size from a shrub to a tree 100 feet tall. The leaves are usually small, rounded or blunt, and grayish, and the flower appears as a tuft of red stamens emerging from close-growing petals. Visitors frequently identify it as a bottlebrush tree due to the close similarity of the two. Both the Lehua and the bottlebrush are in the myrtle family. Legend says that the lehua is a favorite of Pele, goddess of volcanoes, who will cause rain unless an offering is made to her before a lehua flower is picked.

The last ½ mile is steep and requires agility to climb the precipitous ridge, to make your way around thick brush, and to avoid mud holes. But the views from the summit are ample reward for your efforts. You have a sweeping view of the east side, from the town of Waimanalo (lit., "potable water") to the northeast, to Kailua (lit., "two seas") to the north, and along the magnificent Koolau Range extending west. All this, and a plentiful supply of thimbleberries, await the hiker at the summit. Puu Lanipo (lit., "dense peak") (2621 feet elevation) is to the east (right), on the way to the Wiliwilinui Trail.

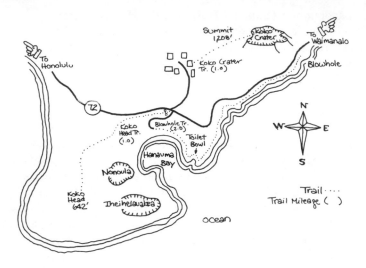

29 Hanauma Bay

Rating: See individual hikes.

Features: Swimming, snorkeling, tidepools, historical sites, blowhole, views of coastal area.

Permission: None.

Hiking Distance & Time: See individual hikes.

Driving Instructions:
From Honolulu (12 miles, ½ hour) drive southeast on H-1, which becomes Route 72, then right on Hanauma Bay Road to parking lot.

Bus Instructions:
From Waikiki at Kalakaua/Monsarrat streets, take the Beach Bus to Hanauma Bay. In the non-summer months (Beach Bus does not operate) take bus #57 ("Kailua/Waimanalo") to Lunalilo Home Road and walk up the hill to the bay.

Introductory Notes: To visit Oahu but fail to hike and swim at Hanauma is a mistake. Hanauma Bay is not only a strikingly beautiful place, but it also offers a variety of hiking experiences.

Koko Head Trail, 1 mile one-way, ½ hour (trail rating: family)

For the protection of your vehicle and for convenience, park in the parking lot at the end of the bay road overlooking Hanauma Bay. To reach the trailhead, walk up the bay road to the highway. A gate across a paved road on your left (west) prevents vehicular travel to the summit of Koko (lit., "blood") Head. Climb through the gate or walk around it for the short hike to the summit. Enchanting views of Hanauma (lit., "curved bay" or "handwrestling bay") Bay and a panorama of the surrounding area are had along the road. Koko Head is a 642-foot-high tuff cone and, according to legend, is the last place on Oahu that Pele, the goddess of volcanoes, attempted to make a home for herself. From the summit, there are good views west to Diamond Head, north to the Koolau Mountain Range and Hawaii Kai (Henry Kaiser's 6000-acre town development.) and northeast to Koko Crater and the coastline around Hanauma. Two small craters are below the summit to the east: Nonoula (lit., "sunburned red") on the left and Iheihelauakea (lit., "wide-leafed ihiihi"—an extinct or unknown plant that may have grown here) on the right. Look directly east and, if it is clear, you should see the island of Molokai some 20 miles across the channel. If you decide to return to the bay by crossing the two craters below, proceed with caution. There is no trail, and the slopes on the bay side of the craters are precipitous and dangerous.

Koko Crater, 1 mile, 1 hour one-way (trail rating: strenuous). Elevation gain 1000 feet.

To reach the trailhead from Hanauma Bay, return to the main highway and take the road opposite the bay road by the sign identifying the "Aloha Hawaii Job Corps Training Center" About ½ mile up this road is the main office, behind which you will find an abandoned inclined railroad that leads directly to the summit.

The railroad ties make a convenient stepped path. Parts of the track are overgrown, so you can expect to have your arms and legs scratched by the brush. Be cautious when you cross over a gulch on a trestle about halfway to the summit. You should also be cautious when walking on the steps and platforms of the abandoned station on the summit, because the wood is broken and rotted in many places. The views from the old powerhouse and the 1208-foot lookout offer a 360° panorama. The Koolau Mountain Range to the north, Diamond Head and Hawaii Kai to the west, Koko Head and Hanauma Bay to the south, and the shoreline to the east treat the eye and calm the spirit after a hard climb. The crater, 100 feet below, contains a botanical garden and bridle trails.

Hanauma Bay to Blowhole, 2 miles one-way, 1½ hours (trail rating: hardy family)

In 1967 Hanauma Bay was declared a marine-life conservation district, which meant that no marine life could be caught here or injured in any manner. Consequently, it is a delightful experience to investigate tidepools or to snorkel and to observe the variety of sea life underwater. Hanauma Bay was once a crater, until the sea broke through the southeast crater wall.

From the beach, hike along the shelf above the water on the east side of the bay. Be alert not only for interesting tidepools but also for waves that may splash onto the shelf. While the danger of being overcome by a wave is slight, it is wise to keep a watchful eye on the water. Be certain to visit the popular "toilet bowl" just beyond the far end of the bay. This interesting feature is a hole about 30 feet in circumference and 10 feet deep which is alternately filled and emptied from beneath as waves come in and recede. Bathers jump or slide into the bowl as it fills. Then, to escape, they scramble out when the water rises to the top of the bowl. Try it. It's different!

From the "toilet bowl" you can climb to the ridge overlooking the bay or follow the coastline around Palea (lit., "brushed aside") Point. From here to the blowhole you are likely to find many local people fishing and snorkeling, so pause to examine their catches and to exchange pleasantries. You will find that a smile and an inquisitive attitude will usually make a friend.

After the first mile, you may choose to hike to the road and to follow it to the blowhole, since the ledge above the water is narrow, and one needs some agility to climb, crawl and jump over the lava while trying to avoid the crashing surf. However, by timing the waves and by using good judgment, you can make it to the blowhole at Halona (lit., "peering place") Point. A blowhole is a narrow vent in the lava through which water is forced by the charging surf. The blowhole at Halona Point "blows" water geysers 30-50 feet into the air, depending on surf conditions. It is a happy terminus to a delightful hike.

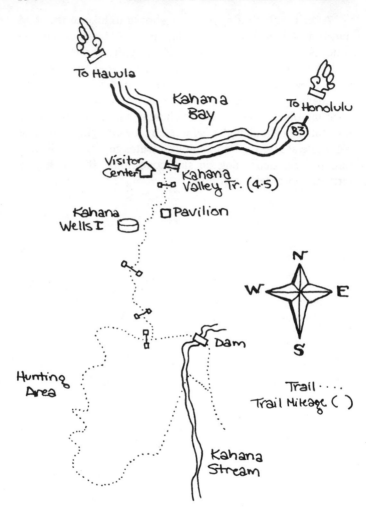

30 Kahana Valley

Rating: Hardy family.

Features: Mountain apples, rose apples, swimming, "living park."

Permission: Division of State Parks.

Hiking Distance & Time: 4.5 miles loop, 2½ hours.

Driving Instructions:

From Honolulu (26 miles, 1 hour) drive northwest on H-1, then right on Route 61 (Pali Highway), then left on Route 83 to Kahana Valley State Park.

Bus Instructions:

From Ala Moana Center take bus #52 ("Kaneohe/ Wahiawa") to Kahana Valley State Park.

Introductory Notes: Kahana (lit., "cutting") Valley State Park has been designated by the state legislature as a "living park." By definition, such a park is intended "to nurture and foster native Hawaiian culture and spread knowledge of its values and ways. . . . This goal is to be achieved by the individuals living there, who will educate the public."

In July 1980 a committee composed of state-park officials and valley residents was formed to develop a program that will be offered to visitors. In the late summer of that year, the state completed a visitor center and a pavilion where some of the 140 valley residents and others will exhibit their skills so that visitors may learn about the traditional Hawaiian way of life in Kahana Valley.

Kahana was once a thriving self-contained community where the people practiced the traditional concept of "ohana"-family units related by blood, marriage and adoption. Ample annual rainfall (from an average of 75 inches along the coast to 300 inches in the back of the valley) sustained the farms, and the ocean provided seafood for the residents. To date, the Bishop Museum has identified 120 small wet terraces and 12 irrigation canals constructed to grow taro.

The Kahana Valley hike is an enjoyable walk for the entire family. Be certain to secure a hiking permit because it will be checked by a caretaker.

On the Trail: From the visitor center, a jeep road leads into the valley for a little over a mile, to a fourth and last gate and the beginning of a hunting area and of a loop trail into the valley. Along this first mile, you pass some residences and

then a couple of demonstration pavilions and public restrooms. Shortly, you pass the "Kahana Well" facility on the
right, then a couple of hunter checking stations, and, just
before the beginning of the loop trail, a papaya grove.

At the last gate, a large sign on the right side inside the
gate identifies the entrance to the hunting area. From this
junction one jeep road goes left for a couple of hundred yards
and ends at the stream and a dam. The road to the right,
bordered by hala trees ends in about ¼ mile and a foot trail
continues into the valley. After crossing a small stream, the
first part of the foot trail passes through a mountain-apple
orchard. In season—usually between June and August
here—these succulent red apples are the highlight of the trip.

Beyond a second small stream crossing, the loop trail is
pleasant and easy to follow until it nears Kahana Stream.
Just before the stream, a number of spur trails go in different
directions. The loop trail (taped in 1981) bears to the left
and descends to the stream. The trails off to the right were
probably made by hunters, by hikers looking for a place to
cross the stream when the water is high, and by people
looking for rose apple (*Eugenia jambos*), an edible, egg-
shaped golden fruit with a rose-water taste and odor. Related
to the mountain apple, the rose-apple tree is an evergreen
with narrow, pointed leaves and large, greenish-white
pompon flowers. At the stream, you should be opposite a
concrete water intake that is under a tangle of branches of a
hau tree. Cross the stream here and crawl under the limbs to
the trail, which becomes clear a short distance beyond the
hau trees. The trail ascends out of this small gulch for 0.2
mile to where it makes a sharp left and descends ½ mile to
the stream and the dam.

Because of the heavy rainfall in the valley, it is not
always easy to make the stream crossing. If you make it, be
alert for the trail-marking tape on trees, which will direct you
to the dam, the gauging station and the swimming holes. If
the water is too high, you may retrace your steps to the
junction at the last gate and from there follow the jeep road
east to the dam.

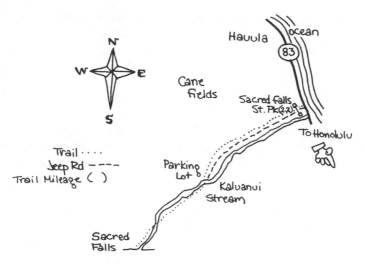

31   Sacred Falls

Rating: Hardy family.

Features: Waterfall, swimming, fruits.

Permission: None.

Hiking Distance & Time: 2.2 miles one-way, 1½ hours.

Driving Instructions:

From Honolulu (28 miles, 1¼ hours) drive northwest on H-1, turn right on Route 61 (Pali Highway), then left on Route 83 to the sign "Sacred Falls State Park" on the left.

Bus Instructions:

From Ala Moana Center take bus #52 ("Kaneohe/ Wahiawa") to sacred Falls State Park.

Introductory Notes: Until recently the hike to Sacred Falls was commercialized, and a fee was charged to park at the end of the cane road. "Kaliuwaa" (lit., "canoe hold" or "canoe leak") is the Hawaiian name for Sacred Falls. Probably the name was changed because "Kaliuwaa" is difficult to pronounce and because "Sacred Falls" sounds more romantic to most tourists. In truth, ancient Hawaiian belief regards the entire valley as sacred to the gods. Legend holds that the pool at the base of the falls is bottomless and leads to another world where a demon lives. The waves in the pool are thought to represent the struggle between the demon and the thrust of the falls, which prevents him from entering this world. Interestingly, another Hawaiian name for the falls and pool is Kaluanua. which literally means "the big pit." To pacify the gods thought to live in the area, believers wrap a stone in a ti leaf and place it along the trail. They believe this act will protect them from falling rocks. Don't miss this hike. Although the trail is usually muddy, it is a fairly easy stroll for the family and offers fruits, picnicking and swimming.

On the Trail: From the trailhead it is 1.2 miles on a cane road to the valley trail. Ahead, you can see the narrow canyon that contains the falls. The road terminates at a large, flat, grassy area that once served as a parking lot. On the left side of this open place, the road becomes a trail, which then crosses a dry stream bed and ascends gently into the canyon. Shortly, the trail reaches Kaluanua Stream, where it is necessary to rock-hop or wade.

In addition to the legends mentioned above, this enchanting, lush island paradise is said to be the home of Kamapuaa (lit., "child of a hog"), who was half human and half swine. Near the end of the valley to the left of the trail, you will cross at the base of a dry fall. This is the site, legend recounts, where Kamapuaa turned himself into a giant hog so that his followers could escape a pursuing army by climbing up his back to safety on the ledge above. The deep impression where water only occasionally falls is said to have been made by the weight and size of his body.

The falls can be heard crashing to the valley floor and can be seen around the next turn in the trail after a stream crossing. The valley walls rise to 1600 feet, but the falls drop only 87 feet. The generous pool at the base is usually muddy and very cold. You might wish to swim or splash in the stream just below the pool. In any event, there is plenty of room for a picnic on the large rocks in this cool, shaded canyon.

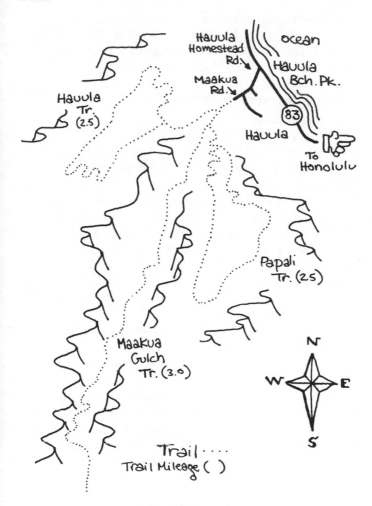

32   Hauula

Rating: See individual hikes.

Features: Views of valley and coastal areas, swimming, waterfall, fruits, native and introduced flora.

Permission: None.

Hiking Distance & Time: See individual hikes.

Driving Instructions:

From Honolulu (30 miles, 1¼ hours) drive northwest on H-1, right on Route 61 (Pali Highway), left on Route 83 to Hauula, left on Hauula Homestead Road opposite the north end of Hauula Beach Park for .2 mile and park at the intersection with Maakua Road.

Bus Instructions:

From Ala Moana Center take bus #52 (Kaneohe/ Wahiawa") to Hauula Beach Park. Cross the highway and walk up Hauula Homestead Road to the trailhead.

Introductory Notes: Three good hikes, camping and swimming await the outdoorsperson in this Hawaiian community. In Hauula (lit., "red hau tree") you will find old Hawaii mixed with the new. You will find local people surf fishing, throwing a net, "talking stories" and having 3-4 generation ohana ("family") picnics on the beach. There are not many tourists who hike these trails, but you are likely to encounter local school children with their teacher or Boy Scouts with their leader.

Hauula Trail, 2.5-mile loop, 1½ hours (trail rating: hardy family). Elevation gain 600 feet.

Walk straight into the woods between the houses on Maakua Road, which becomes a dirt road after the last house. In 200 yards this dirt road becomes mere trail, and 100 yards farther, at a junction, the Maakua Gulch Trail veers left while the less-trod Hauula Trail goes straight ahead. A jeep road turns off to the right shortly before the junction. You pass through some heavy brush, ford a small stream and then switchback up a ridge to where Norfolk Island pines dominate. The fallen needles provide a soft underfooting and make the air aromatic. At midpoint along the ridge, do not take the trail entering on the right but bear left up the ridge. The trail switchbacks up the ridge, traverses Waipilopilo (lit., "smelly water") Gulch, and then ascends along another ridge overlooking Kaipapau (lit., "shallow sea") Valley, from which you have good views of the Koolau Mountain Range, and of the east-side coast line and Hauula.

The route then gently slopes and descends to join the initial part of the trail, on which you retrace your steps.

Maakua Gulch, 3 miles one-way, 3 hours (trail rating: strenuous). 1100 feet elevation gain.

Walk straight into the woods between the houses on Maakua Road, which becomes a dirt road after the last house. In 200 yards this dirt road becomes mere trail, and 100 yards farther, at a junction, the Maakua Gulch Trail veers left while the less trod Hauula Trail goes straight ahead. Just 140 yards farther, you pass the start of the Papali Trail on the left. Maakua Gulch becomes narrower and narrower, and the trail twists and turns along a route that crisscrosses the stream countless times. Be prepared to get wet and to rock-hop throughout the last half of the hike, since the trail is in the streambed there. The narrow canyon and its high, steep walls make this an enchanting hike. Another compensation is the frequent clusters of red mountain apple trees and a good supply of guava trees. The beautiful kukui (*Aleurites moluccana*) tree is common in the gulch. Nicknamed the "candlenut tree," the kukui was a valuable resource until the 20th century. Kukui-nut oil was burned for light, the trunk was used to make canoes if the more durable koa tree was not available, and beautiful and popular leis were made of the nuts. To make a lei, each nut must be sanded, filed and polished to a brilliant luster that is acquired from its own oil. The kukui is also the Hawaii State tree. The hike ends at the base of a small cascade—or, if you're an expert scrambler, the base of a small waterfall just above. At the bottom of the waterfall and the bottom of the cascade are pools large enough for a cooling dip.

Papali, 2.5-mile loop, 2 hours (trail rating: hardy family). 800 feet elevation gain.

Walk straight into the woods between the houses on Maakua Road, which becomes a dirt road after the last house. In 200 yards this dirt road becomes mere trail, and 100 yards farther, at a junction, the less-trod Hauula Trail goes straight ahead but your trail veers left. Just 140 yards past the junction, on the left, is the overgrown start of the Papali (lit., "small cliff or slope") Trail. You have to duck and bend to get through the hau (*Hibiscus tiliaceus*) trees at the trailhead. In the wild, this yellow-flowered hibiscus grows twisting and branching along the ground, forming an impenetrable mass of tangled branches. The lightweight hau wood was used for canoe outriggers, fish floats, adze handles and fence posts. Maakua Stream slowly trickles through the hau grove and must be crossed. The trail then climbs sharply along switchbacks, passing concrete slabs that once supported water tanks. The trail heads toward the mountains for about a mile and then turns east and descends into Papali Gulch and crosses tiny Papali Stream. Although you'll share the scenic stream crossing with mosquitoes, pause in this serene place. Civilization seems a long way off. From here, the trail ascends along the ridge, until it rejoins the earlier trail segment near the concrete slabs. In the last mile of the hike you have outstanding views of Hauula town and north to Laie Point.

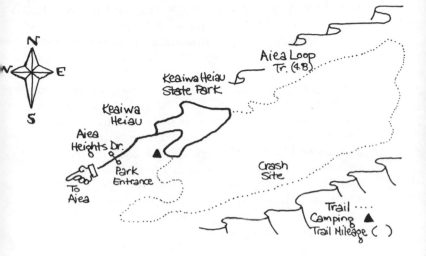

33   Aiea Loop

Rating: Hardy family.

Features: Views of Pearl Harbor, fruits, camping, Keaiwa Heiau.

Permission: Camping permits from Division of State Parks.

Hiking Distance & Time: 4.8-mile loop, 3 hours.

Driving Instructions:

From Honolulu (12 miles, ½ hour) drive northwest on H-1, bear left at sign "Aiea #78," go right at "Aiea" turnoff, follow Moanalua Road downhill to a right turn on Aiea Heights Drive, and go to its end. After entering the park, follow the one-way road to the northeast end of the park and a sign marking the upper Aiea Loop trailhead.

Bus Instructions:

From Ala Moana Center take Bus #11 ("Honolulu/Aiea Heights") to Aiea and to the Kaamilo/Aiea Heights Drive junction. Walk up Aiea Heights Drive to Keaiwa Heiau State Park and to the trailhead.

Introductory Notes: Take time to visit the remains of the heiau (a pre-Christian place of worship) by the park entrance. Keaiwa (lit., "the mystery") Heiau was an ancient healing temple where a priest by the same name was said to have had mysterious healing powers. Keaiwa used the plants grown in the area for medicinal purposes, and instructed novitiates in the art of healing. As is true at so many heiaus in the Islands, little remains of the structures, since they were made mainly of wood and grass.

Keaiwa Heiau State Park offers a good family hiking trail, first-class picnic grounds in a forested setting, and a comfortable campground. The Aiea (lit., "nothocestrum tree") Loop Trail is likely to be crowed on weekends, when local people come to enjoy the park and to hike.

On the Trail: The first part of the trail snakes along the ridge on a wide and well-maintained path where you can identify thin barked eucalyptus, symmetrical Norfolk Island pine and ironwood (*Casuarina equisetifolia*), with its long, thin, drooping, dull green needles. Many of these trees are the result of a reforestation program begun by Thomas McGuire in 1928. The shade from the big trees and the trade winds make this part of the hike both cool and pleasurable.

The trail makes a sharp right turn at 1.6 miles, where a trail to Koolau Ridge departs eastward, and then follows the ridge above North Halawa (lit., "curve") Stream, from which views of the Koolau Mountains and North Halawa Valley are good. The trail descends through a forest of trees, where you will find some native trees, including koa and ohia lehua. At the 3-mile point, look to the right of the trail for the remains of a C-47 cargo plane that crashed in 1943. Just beyond the crash site, a bridle path leads off to the left to Camp Smith and then the loop trail swings to the right and downhill to cross Aiea Stream. Before crossing the stream, you may choose to stroll along a trail to the left that follows the stream. The Aiea Loop trail crosses the stream and then climbs up to the campground and the lower Aiea Loop trailhead, which is just across the grass below the only toilet building in the camping area.

Waimano

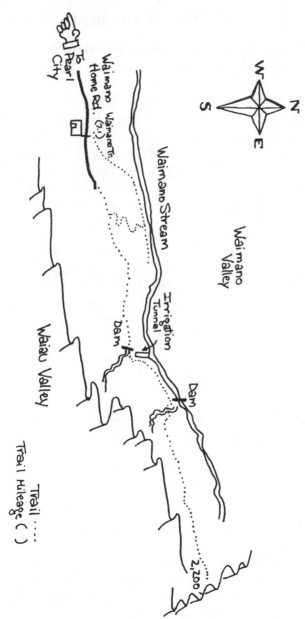

To Pearl City

Waimano Home Rd. (r.r.)

Waimano Tr.

Waimano Stream

Waimano Valley

N
W — E
S

Irrigation Tunnel

Dam

Dam

Waiau Valley

2,200

Trail .....
Trail Mileage ( )

34 Waimano

Rating: Difficult. Elevation gain 1600 feet.

Features: Views from the Koolau Mountain Range, swimming, native and introduced flora.

Permission: None.

Hiking Distance & Time: 7.1 miles one-way, 4 hours.

Driving Instructions:

From Honolulu (14 miles, ½ hour) drive northwest on H-1 to Pearl City (Exit 10), bear right on Moanalua Road to its end, then right on Waimano Home Road (1.7 miles) to the end at a guard shelter. The trailhead is on the left side of the fence.

Bus Instructions:

From Ala Moana Center take Bus #53 (Honolulu-Pacific Palisades) to Pearl City Shopping Center (Kamehameha Highway and Waimano Home Road intersection). Transfer to Pearlridge-Pearl City shuttle bus and take to Komo Mai Drive. Walk up Waimano Home Road to the trailhead.

Introductory Notes: Waimano (lit., "many waters") is one of a number of hikes that take the hiker to viewpoints overlooking the east side of the island from the Koolau Mountain Range.

On the Trail: The trail parallels the fence a short distance and then descends for about ¼ mile to the stream. An abandoned, rusting vehicle just before the stream gives evidence that the trail was originally a jeep road built during World War II. Usually, the trail along the stream is wet and muddy. Some ample swimming holes in the stream provide some relief from the heat and places to clean up, particularly on the return hike. About ½ mile from the trailhead, turn right onto the trail that ascends the south side of the ridge until it meets an old irrigation ditch. The trail to the right at the ditch leads to the now-closed trailhead of what was once called the "Upper Ditch Trail." Go left on the trail paralleling the irrigation ditch until it reaches a dam and an irrigation tunnel after 2 miles. From the tunnel, which is no longer used, the trail switchbacks up to the crest of a ridge overlooking Waimano Stream. For the next mile, the trail follows the ridge above the stream. You can expect to find some generous pools to swim in, if you wish to scramble down the hillside to them. A dam just before the confluence of Waimano Stream and a smaller stream entering from the right marks the point where you start to ascend the ridge that leads to the Koolau crest.

The lower valley contains two of the most noble trees on the island. The kukui, or candlenut tree, a massive tree with maplelike leaves and black, walnut-sized nuts, was one of the most important trees to the island's economy. Kukui-nut oil was burned in stone lamps, the nuts were made into leis and a variety of costume jewelry, and the trunk was used to make canoes. The monkey-pod tree (*Samanea saman*) will commonly grow to 80 feet. It is a symmetrical tree with tiny, delicate pink tufts when in bloom, and tiny fernlike leaflets. From the handsome wood, beautiful and highly prized bowls and trays are made. Both trees as well as the familiar hau tree are conspicuous in this valley.

From the last dam, the trail climbs 1600 feet to the summit, and this is the most difficult section. Since the path here is overgrown in places, it is a good idea to wear long pants and a shirt. Periodically, you will have good views of Waimano Valley to north (left) and of Waiau (lit., "swirling water") Valley to the south (right). However, the highlight of the hike, and the primary reason for making it, is to stand at the crest high above Waihee (lit., "squid liquid") Valley to the east. You will encounter strong winds at the crest. If rain or clouds obstruct your view, be patient, for the wind usually blows the obstruction away quickly.

Manana Valley
Manana Stream
2,660'
Manana Tr.
(6.0)
Komo Mai Dr.
Water
Tank
To
Honolulu
Waimano Valley
N
W   E
S

Trail · · · ·
Trail Mileage ( )

35 Manana

Rating: Difficult. Elevation gain 1700 feet.

Features: Views from the Koolau Mountain Range, native and introduced flora.

Permission: None.

Hiking Distance & Time: 6 miles one-way, 4 hours.

Driving Instructions:

From Honolulu (15 miles, ½ hour) drive northwest on H-1 to Pearl City (Exit 10), bear right on Moanalua Road to its end, then right on Waimano Home Road for 0.7 mile, and finally left on Komo Mai Drive to the end.

Bus Instruction:

From Ala Moana Center take Bus #53 (Honolulu-Pacific Palisades) to Pearl City Shopping Center (Kamehameha Highway and Waimano Home Road intersection). Transfer to Pearlridge-Pearl City Shuttle bus and take to Komo Mai Drive. Walk up Komo Mai Drive to trailhead.

Introductory Notes: The Manana Trail is one of a number of trails that take you to peaks atop the Koolau Mountain Range. This trail is little traveled and is overgrown in places, and should be attempted only by skilled hikers. (It is possible to connect with the Waimano Trail by following the cliffs to the south, but the connecting route is very dangerous and not advised.) Rain and mud are frequently encountered in this relatively pristine place. If you are looking for solitude and for the joys as well as the trials present in a rainforest, then Manana will satisfy you.

On the Trail: A paved pedestrian passageway leads 0.4 mile to a water tank. Strawberry guava is abundant along this part of the trail. From the tank, the Manana Trail steadily climbs 1700 feet to a peak atop the Koolau Range. Eucalyptus, guava and koa trees are abundant along the lower part of the trail, where they are struggling to overcome the ravages of a severe fire in 1972. For your protection, stay on the ridgeline and avoid the side trails, most of which lead to Manana Stream to the north (left) or Waimano Stream to the south. Time permitting, you may wish to hike to Manana Stream for a swim. If so, it would be a good idea to mark your route down so you can follow it back.

In addition to the trees previously noted, look for the majestic sandalwood tree (*Santalum freycinetianum*), with its narrow, pointed, shiny leaves. Once an important source of income for the islands, the wood was exported for use in furniture and for its oil and perfume. In fact, China imported so much sandalwood that the Chinese once called Hawaii the "Sandalwood Islands."

A variety of ferns and low scrub dominate the upper part of the trail and seem to reach out to scratch and cut the legs and arms, so protective clothing is well-advised. Strong winds greet the hiker at the summit, but with any luck the air will be clear, so that the views into Kaalaea (lit., "the ocherous earth") Valley can be enjoyed. A return via the Waimano Trail is possible for the daring and skilled hiker. The 1-mile hike south to it along the cliffs is extremely dangerous, and a miscalculation could drop the hiker 1500 feet or more to the valley below. Caution is well-advised.

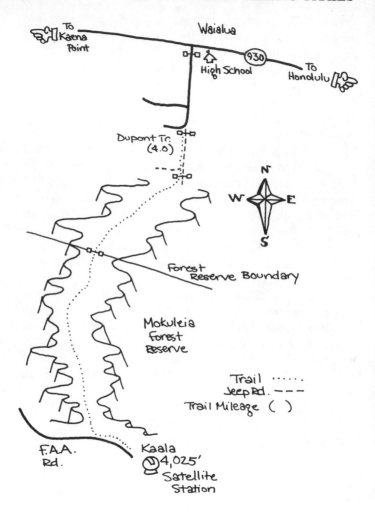

36 Dupont

Rating: Difficult (and dangerous). Elevation gain 3800 feet.

Features: Views from the highest point on Oahu (4025 feet), forest and pasture land, native flora.

Permission: (1) Hiking permit from Division of Forestry. (2) Liability waiver from Waialua Sugar Company.

Hiking Distance & Time: 4 miles one-way, 5 hours.

Driving Instructions:

From Honolulu (30 miles, 1½ hours) drive northwest on H-1, then right on H-2 to end of freeway (completed to Wahiawa at time writing). Continue on Route 99, then bear left on Route 803. At a traffic circle, take Route 930 west to Waialua and to Waialua High School. Go left on a cane road just past the school. Drive 1.5 miles up road and park by the second gate.

Bus Instructions:

From Ala Moana Center take Bus #52 (Honolulu-Wahiawa-Kaneohe) to Wahiawa and to California Ave. Transfer to Bus #72 (Waialua-Haleiwa) and take it to the Goodale Ave./Farrington Highway junction in Waialua. Walk or hitchhike west on the highway to the trailhead.

Introductory Notes: Mt. Kaala (probably, "to hurl stones with a sling") is noteworthy for at least two reasons: it is the highest point on Oahu and the ascent of it is the most difficult hike on the island. The last mile of the hike is very dangerous, and requires skill and a stout heart. Parts of this trail require the hiker to scramble, climb and crawl along narrow ledges with a 2000-foot drop into the valley below. (Ropes have been placed to aid hikers in the most difficult places). If heights are a problem for you, DO NOT attempt this hike. This is not a hike for timid people! You can reach the summit via a longer route on roads.

On the Trail: The Dupont Trail begins beyond the second gate, where the road makes a right turn. Proceed straight ahead on a jeep road a short distance until you reach a gate that secures the pasture land, where the jeep road turns right. From here, Mt. Kaala, distinguished by the white, domed radio and radar installations, is to your front-left, while Kaupakuhale (lit., "house ridgepole or roof") Ridge is to your front-right. You must hike cross-country up Kaupakuhale Ridge. There is no trail until you reach the Forest Reserve boundary 1.3 miles distant. Therefore, you should walk toward the ridge through the pasture land and over a few small hills. What appear to be trails are simply cattle contours, which will lead you in circles if you follow them. A fence and a locked gate on the ridge mark the beginning of the foot trail through the Mokuleia (lit., "isle of abundance") Forest Reserve.

The difference between the pasture and the forest is apparent. The forest part of the trail passes through heavy foliage, which periodically obscures the trail. However, the ridge begins to narrow considerably, and here the danger lies not in losing the trail but in stumbling or sliding off the ridge. A variety of native plants is evident in the forest. Ohia, with its bright red flowers, and hapuu (*Cibotium chamissoi*), or Hawaiian tree fern, are plentiful. The most notable use of the tree fern has been the carving of tikis (carved representation of ancestors) from the trunk. In times of famine, the stems and the core of the trunk have been used for food.

As you ascend, the ridge will alternately narrow and widen. Be cautious and alert, particularly in those places where the footing is composed of loose and brittle volcanic rock. Pause frequently to study the trail ahead and to enjoy the views of the north side of the island and of the deep and startling valleys and gulches on each side of the ridge. The last 1 mile climbs 1800 feet and is the most dangerous part of the hike. Ropes have been placed at the most difficult and the narrowest parts of the ridge. BE CERTAIN to test these ropes to determine whether they will support your weight. Indeed, you may wish to pause and consider returning down the trail rather than risking the difficult ascent ahead.

Abruptly, the trail meets a paved road, which will take you to the summit ¼ mile away. Federal officials do not welcome visitors to the radio and radar facilities at the summit, as numerous "no trespassing" signs attest. Mt. Kaala presides over the island at 4025 feet. The summit is a mile-wide plateau containing a montane bog which has been considerably altered by building over the years. On a clear day, the views of the island, particularly those to the west, are overwhelming. Makaha Valley lies at your feet, and the sweep of the coastline to Kaena Point is sufficient reward for your efforts.

From the summit you may choose to follow the road instead of returning via the trail. It is 8.3 miles to Farrington Highway. If you're lucky, you might get a ride in one of the service vehicles or with the personnel who work at the summit installation. Hawaiian raspberries (*Rubus hawaiiensis*) are abundant along the road, and although the dark berries are edible, they can be rather bitter.

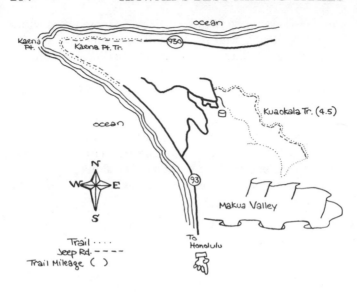

Trail · · · ·
Jeep Rd. − − − −
Trail Mileage ( )

37 Kuaokala

Rating: Strenuous. Elevation gain 500 feet.

Features: Views of mountain and coastal area, fruits, camping.

Permission: Permit to hike and to camp from Division of Forestry.

Hiking Distance & Time: 4½-mile loop, 3 hours.

Driving Instructions:

From Honolulu (41 miles, 2 hours) drive northwest on H-1, which becomes Route 93 when the freeway ends. Drive past Makua town to a military road and a guard shack on the right just before the end of the paved road. Go right on the military road and check in at the guard shack. Drive 2.6 miles on the military road to the designated parking area.

Bus Instructions:

From Ala Moana Center take Bus #51 (Honolulu-Makaha) to the end of the line near the surfing beach north of Makaha. Walk or hitchhike to the military road and guard shack.

Introductory Notes: A good hike, solitude and magnificent views are what you will find in the Kuaokala (lit., "back of the sun") Forest Reserve. The access road is under military jurisdiction, so permits are a must.

On the Trail: The trailhead and the designated parking place are one and the same. If you look back about 100 yards along the road you drove on and then to the left to a water tank, you will see the point at which you will emerge from the loop hike. The route descends on the paved road next to the parking area and continues on a dirt jeep road for 2.8 miles. The paved part of the road is lined with guava trees whose fruit is some of the sweetest I have ever eaten. These lemon-sized fruits are yellow and soft when ripe. The trail makes a number of dips and turns in and out of small gulches which are heavily shaded with eucalyptus, pine, and cypress trees. After about one mile the trail ascends a ridge over open country and reaches a number of points from which panoramas are possible of the saddle area between the two mountain ranges of Oahu, of the Koolau Mountains to the east and of the north shore. These viewpoints are pleasant places to pause. From the second vista point, at a gate and cattle guard, look to the front across a gulch to the ridge at the head of the gulch. You will be hiking along that ridge overlooking Makua Valley. From the second vista point, the trail makes a steep descent and snakes over the gulch's floor before ascending to the ridgeline. Just before the ridge, at the 2.6-mile point at a turnout on the left, the remains of the Kuaokala shack are partly visible through the tall grass. From here, the foot trail is just 0.2 mile. A short distance from the abandoned shack, you reach a four-road junction. Follow the road to the front-right a short distance to a turnout which was once the start of a jeep road and which leads uphill to a group of eucalyptus trees. At this point you have your first view of Makua (lit., "parents") Valley.

The footpath part of the Kuaokala Trail begins to the

right from the viewpoint overlooking Makua Valley and descends west along the north ridge above Makua Valley. After a descent, the trail ascends to a perch 1800 feet above the Makua Valley floor, where views of the valley and the west coast of Oahu are outstanding. Then the trail makes another descent and begins to turn north through open forest. The "golf ball" at the Kaena Point Satellite Tracking Station at the trailhead is now visible. The trail continues a circuitous path through the forest until it reaches a trail junction at the 4.0-mile point. The spur trail straight ahead ascends a short distance to a viewpoint, and the main trail turns to the right. Take the spur trail and enjoy the views. It is a good lunch spot. Return to the main trail and follow it to the water tank. Then walk down the paved road from the tank to the main road and turn right to reach the trailhead.

Appendix

For Maui, Lanai, and Molokai

(write to)
Superintendent
Haleakala National Park
P.O. Box 537
Makawao, Maui 96768

1. park information
2. crater cabin reservations

(in person)
Haleakala National Park
  Headquarters
P.O. Box 369
Tel. 572-9306

1. park information
2. crater camping permits
3. crater cabin keys and information

Division of State Parks
P.O. Box 1049
State Office Building
Wailuku, Maui 96793
Tel. 244-4354

1. camping permits for state parks
2. cabin rental reservations

Department of Parks and
  Recreation
War Memorial Gym
Kaahumanu Ave.
Wailuku, Maui 96793
Tel. 244-5514

1. camping permits for county campgrounds

Division of Forestry
P.O. Box 1015
Wailuku, Maui 96793
Tel. 244-4352

1. hiking permission for Kanaha Bird Sanctuary

Maui County Visitor's
  Association
P.O. Box 1738
Kahului, Maui 96732
Tel. 871-8691

1. general tourist information

Department of Parks &
  Recreation
P.O. Box 526
Kaunakakai, Molokai 96748

1. camping permits for One Alii (Molokai)

Koele Company
Lanai City, Hawaii 96763
Tel. 565-6661

1. camping permits for Hulopoe Bay

For Oahu

Division of State Parks
1151 Punchbowl St.
Room 310
Honolulu, Oahu 96813
Tel. 548-7455

1. camping permit for state park

Zions Securities Corp.
Laie Shopping Center
55-510 Kamehameha Highway
Laie, Oahu 96762
Tel. 293-9201

1. camping permit for Kakela and Hukilau, private campgrounds.

Division of Forestry
1151 Punchbowl St., Room 325
Honolulu, Oahu 96813
Tel. 548-2861

1. hiking permits
2. camping and shelter use permits

Waialua Sugar Co.
Waialua, Oahu 96786
Tel. 637-4436

1. access permit

Department of Parks and
   Recreation
Honolulu Municipal Building
Honolulu, Oahu 96813
Tel. 955-3711

1. camping permits

OR from Satellite City Halls:

Kaneohe
46-018 Kam Hwy.
Kaneohe, Oahu 96744
Tel. 235-4571

Kalihi
1865 Kam IV Road
Honolulu, Oahu 96819
Tel. 847-4688

Kailua
302 Kuulei Rd.
Kailua, Oahu 96734
Tel. 261-8575

Hawaii Kai
2nd Floor
Koko Marina Shopping Center
Honolulu, Oahu 96825
Tel. 395-4418

Wahiawa
830 California Ave.
Wahiawa, Oahu 96786
Tel. 621-0791

Ewa
91-923 Ft. Weaver Road
Ewa Beach, Oahu 96706
Tel. 689-7914

Waianae
85-555 Farington Hwy.
Waianea, Oahu 96792
Tel. 696-6371

Beretania
1290 Aala St.
Honolulu, Oahu 96817
Tel. 523-2405

Waipahu
Waipahu Shopping Plaza
Tel. 671-5638

Hauula
Hauula Kai Shopping Center
54-316 Kam Hwy.
Tel. 293-8551

For Hawaii

Superintendent
Hawaii Volcanoes National
   Park
Hawaii 96718
Tel. 967-7311

1. park information
2. hiking permits
3. camping permits—where
   applicable

Volcano House
Hawaii Volcanoes National
   Park
Hawaii 96718

1. rental camper cabins at
   Namakani Paio
2. hotel rooms at Volcano
   House

Department of Parks &
   Recreation
County of Hawaii
25 Aupuni Street
Hilo HI 96720
Tel. 961-8311

1. camping permits for county
   parks

Division of State Parks
State of Hawaii
P.O. Box 936
75 Aupuni Street
Hilo HI 96720
Tel. 961-7200

1. camping permits for state
   parks
2. hunting and fishing
   requirements

Hawaii County Transit System
25 Aupuni Street
Hilo HI 96720
Tel. 961-8343

1. bus information and
   schedules

Hawaii Visitors Bureau
180 Kinoole Street
Hilo HI 96720

1. general travel information

For Kauai

Division of State Parks
State Building, Room 306
3060 Eiwa St.
P.O. Box 1671
Lihue, Hawaii 96766

1. camping permits for state
   parks and for Kalalau Trail

County of Kauai
Portable Building #5
4191 Hardy St.
   (behind Convention Hall)
Lihue, Hawaii 96766

1. pick up camping permits for
   county parks

County of Kauai
Parks & Recreation
4396 Rice St.
Lihue, Hawaii 96766

1. mail for permits

Division of Forestry
State Building, Room 208
3060 Eiwa St.
Lihue, Hawaii 96766

1. hiking information on Kauai

Kokee Lodge
P.O. Box 819
Kekaha, Hawaii 96752

1. housekeeping cabin information and reservations

Hawaii Visitor's Bureau
4444 Rice St.
Lihue, Hawaii 96766

1. general travel information

Bob's Bargain Rentals
P.O. Box 3208
Lihue, Hawaii 96766

1. camping equipment for rent

Hanalei Camping &
   Backpacking
1245 Hanalei
Hanalei, Hawaii 96714

1. camping equipment for rent

Beach Boy Campers
P.O. Box 3208
Lihue, Hawaii 96766

1. campers for rent

Other Books From Wilderness Press

Wilderness Press publishes many other fine outdoor books. The complete list is below. Write for a free catalog.

Arizona Trails
Backpackers Sourcebook
Backpacking Basics
Bicycling in Hawaii
Hawaiian Camping
Hiking Hawaii
Hiking Kauai
Hiking Maui
Hiking Oahu
Huckleberry Country
Lassen Volcanic National Park
Marble Mountain Wilderness
A Pacific Crest Odyssey
Point Reyes
San Bernardino Mountain Trails

Sierra Nevada Flora
Sierra North
Sierra South
The Anza-Borrego Desert Region
The Boundary Waters Canoe Area
The John Muir Trail
The Pacific Crest Trail
The Tahoe Sierra
The Tahoe-Yosemite Trail
Trails of the Angeles
The Vertical World of Yosemite
Waxing for Cross-Country Skiing
Wild Food Plants of the Sierra
Yosemite Climber
Yosemite National Park

Desolation Wilderness and the South Lake Tahoe Basin
Guide to the Golden Gate National Recreation Area
Nordic Touring and Cross-Country Skiing
Outdoor Guide to the San Francisco Bay Area
Self-Propelled in the Southern Sierra
The Cross-Country Ski, Cook, Look and Pleasure Book
The Sawtooth National Recreation Area

PLUS hiking guides to all the 15-minute quadrangles in the High Sierra, such as **Tuolumne Meadows**, **Mineral King** and **Mt. Whitney**.

Wilderness Press

2440 bancroft way · berkeley, california 94704

Index